THE TIME-SAVING

MEDITERRANEAN DIET COOKBOOK FOR BUSY BEGINNERS

2100 Days of No-Stress Recipes for Quick and Healthy Meals Ready in 30 Minutes or Less

Dining Out Mediterranean Way Guidebook Included

Daniel Ortiz

TABLE OF CONTENTS

Introduction

Embark on a culinary journey infused with the vibrant flavors, wholesome traditions, and healthful essence of the Mediterranean. In this culinary odyssey, we explore the Mediterranean Diet—a lifestyle rooted in centuries of culinary wisdom and cultural richness. Beyond a mere collection of recipes, this book serves as your guide to understanding and embracing the core principles that define the Mediterranean way of life.

Discover the Origins and Cultural Significance, delving into the historical tapestry that weaves together the diverse communities bordering the Mediterranean Sea. Uncover the Key Principles of the Mediterranean Lifestyle, guiding you through a holistic approach to well-being that extends beyond the plate. Explore the Health Benefits and Scientific Backing, where we unravel the secrets behind the diet's reputation as a powerhouse of nutrition and longevity.

As we navigate this culinary expedition, we'll encounter an array of delectable recipes meticulously curated to cater to your modern, time-conscious lifestyle. From soulful breakfasts to enticing appetizers, wholesome main courses, and indulgent desserts, each recipe is crafted with a commitment to simplicity, flavor, and the nutritional essence that defines the Mediterranean way.

Immerse yourself in the art of Mediterranean cooking, where fresh, seasonal ingredients become your palette, and every meal is a celebration of life, health, and community.

Whether you're a seasoned home cook or just starting on your culinary adventure, this cookbook invites you to savor the delights of the Mediterranean Diet and embrace a lifestyle that transcends the boundaries of a meal—it's a journey of nourishment, vitality, and joy. Welcome to a world where food is not just sustenance but a symphony of taste, tradition, and well-being.

Origins and Cultural Significance

In the rich tapestry of the Mediterranean, the origins of the celebrated diet are intertwined with the history, geography, and diverse cultures that have flourished along its shores. Our journey begins in ancient times, where the cradle of civilization nurtured a culinary tradition that transcended sustenance, evolving into a way of life. The Mediterranean Diet, as we know it today, draws inspiration from the agricultural practices, culinary techniques, and communal values that have been passed down through generations.

The roots of this dietary marvel can be traced back to the ancient civilizations of Greece and Rome, where olives, grains, and an abundance of fresh produce laid the foundation for a diet that prioritized simplicity and wholesomeness. As we traverse the landscapes of Italy, Greece, Morocco, Spain, and Lebanon, each region contributes its own unique flavors and culinary nuances to the collective Mediterranean table. The diverse climates, fertile soils, and the bounty of the sea converge to create a mosaic of ingredients that form the backbone of this nutritional philosophy.

Cultural significance is woven into every meal, as the act of dining becomes a celebration of life, family, and community. The

Mediterranean Diet reflects a holistic approach to sustenance, emphasizing not just what is consumed but the manner in which it is shared. From the lively markets of Marrakech, where the aroma of spices hangs in the air, to the sun-kissed vineyards of Tuscany, where the art of winemaking is a testament to tradition, the cultural tapestry of the Mediterranean unfolds in every dish.

The olive tree, an emblematic figure in this narrative, epitomizes the enduring connection between the people of the Mediterranean and the land they inhabit. The olive branch, an ancient symbol of peace, adorns tables from Athens to Beirut, underlining the communal spirit that accompanies each meal. The rituals of harvesting olives and pressing them into oil echo through the ages, serving as a tangible link to the past and a source of nourishment for the future.

As we explore the culinary customs of the Mediterranean, we encounter the reverence for seasonality and local produce. From the sun-ripened tomatoes of the Italian countryside to the aromatic herbs of the Greek hillsides, the diet mirrors the ebb and flow of nature. The reliance on fresh, unprocessed ingredients not only enhances the flavors but also aligns with a sustainable and ecologically conscious way of life.

In essence, the origins and cultural significance of the Mediterranean Diet are rooted in a profound respect for the land, a deep appreciation for the interconnectedness of communities, and an enduring commitment to the timeless rituals of shared meals. Through this exploration, we unearth the stories embedded in each recipe, the wisdom passed from one generation to the next, and the enduring legacy of a diet that transcends culinary boundaries to become a way of life.

Key Principles of the Mediterranean Lifestyle

At the heart of the Mediterranean Diet lies a set of principles that extend beyond the mere selection of foods, encapsulating a holistic lifestyle deeply rooted in tradition and well-being. The Mediterranean lifestyle is a testament to the symbiotic relationship between nourishment, physical activity, and the profound connection to one's surroundings. These key principles form the pillars upon which individuals in the Mediterranean region have not just thrived but have also cultivated a profound sense of balance and vitality.

Central to this lifestyle is the recognition that food is not just fuel; it is a source of pleasure, a catalyst for social engagement, and a cornerstone of overall health. Embracing the Mediterranean way involves savoring the sensory experience of each meal, from the vibrant colors on the plate to the aromas that evoke memories of sun-drenched landscapes. The act of eating is a deliberate and unhurried affair, fostering a mindful approach that allows for the appreciation of every bite.

Physical activity is seamlessly integrated into the fabric of daily life, with a focus on staying active rather than adhering to strict exercise regimens. From leisurely strolls along the cobblestone streets of coastal villages to engaging in outdoor activities that celebrate the diverse landscapes, the Mediterranean lifestyle places a premium on movement as a source of joy and vitality. This harmonious blend of movement and nourishment is a fundamental aspect of the lifestyle, contributing not only to physical well-being but also to mental and emotional equilibrium.

A profound respect for the seasons and the natural rhythms of life underscores the third principle of the Mediterranean lifestyle. The ebb and flow of the agricultural calendar influence not only the availability of fresh produce but also the culinary choices made by individuals. Seasonal, locally sourced ingredients take precedence, ensuring that meals are not only flavorful but also aligned with the cycles of nature. This mindful approach to eating not only supports the body's nutritional needs but also fosters a sense of harmony with the environment.

Furthermore, the Mediterranean lifestyle places a strong emphasis on the conviviality of shared meals. Dining is viewed as a communal experience, a time to gather with loved ones, and a means of strengthening social bonds. The act of breaking bread together goes beyond sustenance; it becomes a vehicle for connection, conversation, and the creation of lasting memories. This communal aspect of meals reinforces a sense of belonging and reinforces the interdependence of individuals within a community.

In essence, the key principles of the Mediterranean lifestyle extend beyond dietary choices to encompass a broader philosophy of living. It is a lifestyle that honors the interconnectedness of nourishment, movement, and community, weaving together a tapestry of well-being that has stood the test of time. Through embracing these principles, individuals can not only adopt a healthful approach to eating but also cultivate a richer, more vibrant way of life inspired by the timeless traditions of the Mediterranean.

Health Benefits and Scientific Backing

The Mediterranean Diet is not just a culinary delight; it is a science-backed prescription for robust health and longevity. The profound health benefits associated with this dietary pattern have sparked considerable interest among researchers and health professionals, leading to a wealth of scientific studies that validate its positive impact on well-being. Beyond the tantalizing flavors and diverse culinary experiences, the Mediterranean Diet stands as a testament to the symbiotic relationship between food and health.

Scientific inquiry has consistently affirmed that the Mediterranean Diet is associated with a myriad of health advantages, ranging from cardiovascular well-being to cognitive function. One of its primary virtues lies in the emphasis on heart-healthy fats, particularly those found in olive oil and fatty fish. These monounsaturated fats have been linked to a reduction in the risk of heart disease, thanks to their ability to lower levels of LDL cholesterol while promoting the health of blood vessels.

The abundance of fruits and vegetables in the Mediterranean Diet contributes not only to its vibrant flavors but also to a wealth of phytonutrients and antioxidants. These bioactive compounds play a pivotal role in combating oxidative stress and inflammation, both of which are implicated in the development of chronic diseases. Numerous studies have underscored the diet's potential to reduce inflammation, offering protective effects against conditions such as diabetes, certain cancers, and neurodegenerative disorders.

Moreover, the Mediterranean Diet has emerged as a champion in the realm of weight management. Its nutrient-dense and fiber-rich composition contribute to a sense of satiety, reducing the likelihood of overeating. The incorporation of whole grains, legumes, and lean proteins further supports weight maintenance and metabolic health.

Beyond the physical realm, the Mediterranean Diet has garnered attention for its impact on cognitive function and mental well-being. Research suggests that the consumption of nutrient-rich foods, particularly those rich in omega-3 fatty acids, may contribute to a lower risk of cognitive decline and neurodegenerative diseases. The diet's emphasis on antioxidants and anti-inflammatory foods also extends its protective effects to mental health, potentially reducing the risk of depression and enhancing overall mood.

In essence, the scientific underpinnings of the Mediterranean Diet affirm that it is not merely a cultural culinary tradition but a potent prescription for a healthful and vibrant life. The convergence of centuries-old dietary wisdom with modern scientific validation positions the Mediterranean Diet as a beacon of preventive medicine, offering a roadmap to a life marked by vitality, resilience, and enduring well-being.

Foods to Embrace in the Mediterranean Diet

At the heart of the Mediterranean Diet's allure lies a palette of wholesome, nutrient-dense foods that not only satiate the senses but also form the cornerstone of a healthful lifestyle. The diet's celebrated array of foods is a testament to the rich agricultural tapestry that graces the Mediterranean region, offering a symphony of flavors, colors, and textures that make each meal a culinary masterpiece.

Fruits and Vegetables: The Vibrant Essence of the Diet

Central to the Mediterranean Diet is the generous inclusion of fruits and vegetables, a cornerstone that not only defines its nutritional profile but also imparts a burst of vibrant colors to every plate. Laden with an assortment of vitamins, minerals, and antioxidants, these plant-based marvels contribute to a myriad of health benefits. From the robust reds of tomatoes to the lush greens of leafy vegetables and the deep purples of berries, each hue represents a unique set of phytonutrients that fortify the body against various ailments.

The Mediterranean tradition recognizes the seasonal ebbs and flows of produce, encouraging individuals to savor the ripest fruits and vegetables each season brings. This not only ensures optimal freshness and flavor but also aligns with the diet's sustainable ethos, fostering a connection between the eater and the land.

Whole Grains: The Sustaining Pillars

Whole grains form another fundamental pillar of the Mediterranean Diet, offering a rich tapestry of options such as farro, bulgur, and whole wheat. Unlike their refined counterparts, whole grains retain the bran and germ, providing a wealth of fiber, vitamins, and minerals. This not only promotes digestive health but also contributes to sustained energy levels, making whole grains a valuable asset in the prevention of chronic diseases, including heart disease and type 2 diabetes.

The Mediterranean predilection for grains extends beyond bread and pasta to include ancient grains like quinoa and barley, diversifying the nutrient intake and introducing unique textures and flavors to the diet. This broad spectrum of grains not only enhances the culinary experience but also underscores the diet's commitment to variety and balance.

Healthy Fats: The Elixir of Longevity

A distinctive feature of the Mediterranean Diet is its liberal use of heart-healthy fats, with extra virgin olive oil taking center stage. This liquid gold not only adds a distinctive flavor to dishes but also serves as a linchpin in the diet's health-promoting effects. Rich in monounsaturated fats and antioxidant compounds, olive oil has been associated with a reduced risk of cardiovascular diseases and inflammation.

In addition to olive oil, the diet embraces other sources of healthy fats, including nuts, seeds, and fatty fish. Almonds, walnuts, and flaxseeds contribute not only to the diet's satiating quality but also deliver a payload of omega-3 fatty acids, supporting brain health and reducing inflammation. Fatty fish, such as salmon and mackerel, further amplify the diet's omega-3 content, providing a delicious means to protect against heart disease and foster overall well-being.

Lean Proteins: The Culinary Alchemy

Proteins in the Mediterranean Diet are sourced from a variety of lean and plant-based options, showcasing the diet's versatility and adaptability. Legumes, such as chickpeas and lentils, take center stage, providing an excellent source of protein, fiber, and a host of essential nutrients. These plant-based powerhouses not only contribute to satiety but

also impart a rich and hearty character to many traditional Mediterranean dishes.

Fish and poultry, prepared with minimal processing and adorned with fragrant herbs and spices, offer a lean and delectable source of protein. The diet's affinity for fish, especially varieties rich in omega-3 fatty acids, adds another layer of cardiovascular protection and elevates the culinary experience.

Herbs and Spices: The Flavorful Tapestry

No exploration of the Mediterranean Diet is complete without delving into the aromatic realm of herbs and spices. Fresh herbs like basil, oregano, and rosemary, along with spices such as cumin and coriander, infuse dishes with a medley of flavors, eliminating the need for excessive salt and unhealthy condiments.

Beyond their culinary appeal, herbs and spices contribute to the diet's healthful profile. Many of these aromatic additions boast anti-inflammatory and antioxidant properties, enhancing the diet's potential to combat chronic diseases. The Mediterranean tradition recognizes the medicinal value of these culinary companions, transforming each meal into a holistic celebration of health and flavor.

In essence, the foods to embrace in the Mediterranean Diet paint a portrait of a culinary tapestry that transcends mere sustenance. It is a canvas where each ingredient plays a vital role not only in crafting delectable meals but also in fostering a culture of well-being and longevity. Through the harmonious marriage of fruits, vegetables, whole grains, healthy fats, lean proteins, and a symphony of herbs and spices, the Mediterranean Diet emerges not just as a dietary choice but as a holistic lifestyle that beckons individuals to savor the joys of wholesome living.

Foods to Limit or Avoid in the Mediterranean Diet

In navigating the Mediterranean Diet, an equal emphasis is placed on not just what to include but also on mindful moderation and conscious choices when it comes to certain foods. The diet's wisdom lies not only in the celebration of healthful options but also in the discerning exclusion of items that may undermine its core principles. Understanding the foods to limit or avoid is crucial in unlocking the full potential of this dietary paradigm, promoting overall well-being and mitigating the risk of various lifestyle-related diseases.

Red and Processed Meats: The Delicate Balance

While the Mediterranean Diet does not categorically eliminate red and processed meats, it advocates for their consumption in moderation. Recognizing the potential health risks associated with excessive intake of red and processed meats, the diet encourages a balanced approach. Infrequent indulgence in lean cuts of red meat and processed meats allows for the enjoyment of these flavors without compromising the diet's overarching commitment to cardiovascular health.

Refined Grains and Sugars: Navigating the Carbohydrate Landscape

Refined grains and sugars, often vilified for their association with various health issues, find limited space in the Mediterranean Diet. The diet favors whole grains over their refined counterparts, recognizing the inherent nutritional value present in the complete grain structure. By minimizing the consumption of white bread, sugary cereals, and processed snacks, individuals following the Mediterranean Diet cultivate a more stable blood sugar profile, promoting sustained energy levels and reducing the risk of diabetes.

Processed Foods: A Detour from Nature's Bounty

A pivotal tenet of the Mediterranean Diet is the preference for whole, minimally processed foods over their heavily processed counterparts. Convenience-driven processed foods, often laden with preservatives, additives, and excessive sodium, can compromise the diet's healthful essence. By steering clear of pre-packaged meals, frozen dinners, and snack items with lengthy ingredient lists, adherents of the Mediterranean Diet prioritize the nutritional integrity of their meals, fostering a deeper connection with the natural bounty of the region.

Excessive Dairy: Navigating Dairy's Role

While dairy products do find a place in the Mediterranean Diet, the emphasis is on moderation and mindful selection. High-fat dairy options, such as whole milk and creamy cheeses, are approached with restraint. The diet encourages the consumption of nutrient-dense alternatives like Greek yogurt and feta cheese, which not only contribute to the diet's protein content but also offer a rich tapestry of vitamins and minerals.

In adopting the Mediterranean Diet, individuals embark on a journey that not only celebrates the abundance of nourishing foods but also acknowledges the importance of balance. By limiting or avoiding certain items, adherents of the diet actively shape their eating habits to align with the diet's overarching goal –

promoting longevity, enhancing vitality, and safeguarding against chronic diseases. This nuanced approach to food selection is emblematic of the Mediterranean lifestyle's holistic philosophy, where every culinary choice becomes a conscious step towards optimal health and well-being.

BREAKFAST

Mediterranean Avocado Toast

Servings: 2
Cooking Time: 10 minutes

Ingredients:
- 2 slices whole-grain bread
- 1 ripe avocado
- 1 tablespoon extra-virgin olive oil
- 1 small garlic clove, minced
- 1 tablespoon lemon juice
- Salt and pepper to taste
- 1 medium tomato, sliced
- 2 tablespoons crumbled feta cheese
- 1 tablespoon chopped fresh basil

Instructions:
1. Toast the whole-grain bread slices to your liking.
2. While the bread is toasting, mash the ripe avocado in a bowl. Add minced garlic, lemon juice, olive oil, salt, and pepper. Mix until well combined.
3. Spread the mashed avocado evenly over the toasted bread slices.
4. Top each slice with tomato slices, crumbled feta cheese, and chopped fresh basil.
5. Season with an extra drizzle of olive oil, salt, and pepper if desired.
6. Serve immediately and enjoy this Mediterranean twist on classic avocado toast.

Nutritional Values (per serving):
- Calories: 250
- Fat: 15g
- Carbs: 25g

- Protein: 6g

Greek Yogurt Parfait with Fresh Berries

Servings: 2
Cooking Time: 10 minutes

Ingredients:
- 1 cup Greek yogurt
- 1 cup mixed fresh berries (strawberries, blueberries, raspberries)
- 2 tablespoons honey
- 1/2 cup granola
- 1/4 cup chopped nuts (almonds or walnuts)
- Fresh mint leaves for garnish

Instructions:
1. In two serving glasses or bowls, spoon a layer of Greek yogurt at the bottom.
2. Add a layer of mixed fresh berries on top of the yogurt.
3. Drizzle one tablespoon of honey over each parfait.
4. Sprinkle granola evenly over the berries.
5. Add a layer of chopped nuts.
6. Repeat the layers until the glasses are filled.
7. Garnish with fresh mint leaves.
8. Serve immediately and enjoy your delightful Greek Yogurt Parfait with Fresh Berries!

Nutritional Values (Per Serving):
- Calories: 350
- Fat: 12g
- Carbs: 45g
- Protein: 15g

Shakshuka with Feta

Servings: 4
Cooking Time: 25 minutes

Ingredients:
- 2 tablespoons olive oil
- 1 onion, diced
- 2 bell peppers, diced
- 2 cloves garlic, minced
- 1 teaspoon ground cumin
- 1 teaspoon ground paprika
- 1/2 teaspoon ground cayenne pepper (adjust to taste)
- 1 can (28 ounces) crushed tomatoes
- Salt and black pepper to taste
- 4-6 large eggs
- 1/2 cup crumbled feta cheese
- Fresh parsley, chopped, for garnish

Instructions:
1. Heat olive oil in a large skillet over medium heat. Add diced onion and bell peppers; sauté until softened.
2. Stir in minced garlic, ground cumin, ground paprika, and ground cayenne pepper; cook for an additional 2 minutes.
3. Pour in the crushed tomatoes and season with salt and black pepper. Simmer for about 10-15 minutes until the sauce thickens.
4. Create small wells in the sauce and crack the eggs into them. Cover and cook until the eggs are set to your liking.
5. Sprinkle crumbled feta over the top and garnish with fresh parsley.
6. Serve immediately, spooning the shakshuka onto plates.

Nutritional Values (Per Serving):
- Calories: 220
- Fat: 14g
- Carbs: 18g
- Protein: 8g

Spinach and Feta Omelette

Servings: 2
Cooking Time: 15 minutes

Ingredients:
- 4 large eggs
- 1 cup fresh spinach, chopped
- 1/2 cup feta cheese, crumbled
- 1/4 cup red bell pepper, diced
- 1/4 cup red onion, finely chopped
- Salt and pepper to taste
- 1 tablespoon olive oil

Instructions:
1. In a bowl, whisk together the eggs until well beaten. Season with salt and pepper.
2. Heat olive oil in a non-stick skillet over medium heat.
3. Add red bell pepper and red onion to the skillet. Sauté until softened.
4. Add chopped spinach to the skillet and cook until wilted.
5. Pour the beaten eggs over the vegetables evenly, allowing them to set around the edges.
6. Sprinkle crumbled feta cheese over one half of the omelette.
7. Carefully fold the omelette in half using a spatula.
8. Cook for an additional 2-3 minutes until the eggs are fully set and the cheese is melted.
9. Slide the omelette onto a plate, cut in half, and serve immediately.

Nutritional Values (per serving):
- Calories: 280
- Fat: 20g
- Carbs: 4g
- Protein: 18g

Olive and Tomato Focaccia

Servings:8
Cooking Time: 30 minutes
Ingredients:

- 1 pound pizza dough
- 2 tablespoons olive oil
- 1 cup cherry tomatoes, halved
- 1/2 cup Kalamata olives, pitted and sliced
- 2 cloves garlic, minced
- 1 teaspoon dried oregano
- Salt and black pepper to taste
- 1/4 cup fresh basil, chopped (for garnish)

Instructions:

1. Preheat the oven to 425°F (220°C). Roll out the pizza dough on a baking sheet.
2. Drizzle olive oil over the dough, spreading it evenly with your hands.
3. Press halved cherry tomatoes and sliced Kalamata olives into the dough.
4. Sprinkle minced garlic, dried oregano, salt, and black pepper over the top.
5. Bake in the preheated oven for 20-25 minutes or until the crust is golden and crispy.
6. Remove from the oven and let it cool for a few minutes.
7. Garnish with chopped fresh basil.
8. Slice and serve warm.

Nutritional Values (per serving):

- Calories: 180
- Fat: 8g
- Carbs: 24g
- Protein: 4g

Whole Wheat Mediterranean Pancakes

Servings:4
Cooking Time: 20 minutes
Ingredients:

- 1 cup whole wheat flour
- 1 tablespoon baking powder
- 1/2 teaspoon salt
- 1 cup milk
- 1 large egg
- 2 tablespoons olive oil
- 1 tablespoon honey
- 1 teaspoon vanilla extract
- 1/2 cup Greek yogurt
- Fresh mixed berries for topping

Instructions:

1. In a bowl, whisk together whole wheat flour, baking powder, and salt.
2. In another bowl, combine milk, egg, olive oil, honey, and vanilla extract.
3. Pour the wet ingredients into the dry ingredients and stir until just combined.
4. Heat a griddle or non-stick skillet over medium heat.
5. Pour 1/4 cup of batter onto the griddle for each pancake.
6. Cook until bubbles form on the surface, then flip and cook until golden brown.
7. Serve pancakes topped with a dollop of Greek yogurt and fresh mixed berries.

Nutritional Values (per serving):

- Calories: 280
- Fat: 10g
- Carbs: 38g
- Protein: 8g

Fig and Walnut Overnight Oats

Servings:2
Prep Time: 10 minutes
Chill Time: Overnight
Ingredients:

- 1 cup old-fashioned oats
- 1 cup almond milk
- 1/2 cup Greek yogurt
- 2 tablespoons honey
- 1/4 cup chopped dried figs
- 1/4 cup chopped walnuts
- 1/2 teaspoon vanilla extract
- Pinch of cinnamon

Instructions:

1. In a jar, combine oats, almond milk, Greek yogurt, honey, dried figs, walnuts, vanilla extract, and cinnamon.
2. Stir well to ensure everything is evenly distributed.
3. Cover the jar with a lid and refrigerate overnight.
4. In the morning, give the oats a good stir and add a splash of almond milk if needed.
5. Top with additional chopped figs and walnuts before serving.

Nutritional Values (per serving):
- Calories: 350
- Fat: 14g
- Carbs: 48g
- Protein: 10g

Mediterranean Egg Muffins

Servings:4
Prep Time: 15 minutes
Cook Time: 15 minutes
Ingredients:
- 6 large eggs
- 1/4 cup diced tomatoes
- 1/4 cup chopped spinach
- 1/4 cup crumbled feta cheese
- 2 tablespoons chopped black olives
- 1 tablespoon chopped fresh basil
- Salt and pepper to taste

Instructions:

1. Preheat the oven to 350°F (175°C). Grease a muffin tin.
2. In a bowl, whisk together eggs, tomatoes, spinach, feta cheese, black olives, basil, salt, and pepper.
3. Pour the egg mixture evenly into the muffin cups.
4. Bake for 15 minutes or until the eggs are set.
5. Allow the muffins to cool slightly before removing them from the tin.
6. Serve warm and enjoy a delightful Mediterranean breakfast!

Nutritional Values (per serving):
- Calories: 130
- Fat: 9g
- Carbs: 3g
- Protein: 9g

Quinoa Breakfast Bowl with Almonds and Honey

Servings:2
Prep Time: 10 minutes
Cook Time: 15 minutes
Ingredients:
- 1/2 cup quinoa, rinsed
- 1 cup almond milk
- 1/4 cup sliced almonds
- 1 tablespoon honey
- 1/2 teaspoon cinnamon
- Fresh berries for topping

Instructions:

1. In a saucepan, combine quinoa and almond milk. Bring to a boil, then reduce heat, cover, and simmer for 15 minutes or until quinoa is cooked.
2. Fluff the quinoa with a fork and divide it into serving bowls.
3. Drizzle honey over the quinoa, sprinkle with sliced almonds, and add a dash of cinnamon.
4. Top with fresh berries of your choice.
5. Stir gently and enjoy this nutritious and delicious Mediterranean breakfast bowl!

Nutritional Values (per serving):
- Calories: 320
- Fat: 10g
- Carbs: 50g
- Protein: 8g

Greek-style Breakfast Burrito

Servings:2
Prep Time: 15 minutes
Cook Time: 10 minutes

Ingredients:

- 4 large eggs
- 1/2 cup cherry tomatoes, halved
- 1/4 cup crumbled feta cheese
- 2 whole wheat tortillas
- 1/4 cup Kalamata olives, sliced
- 1/4 cup fresh spinach, chopped
- Tzatziki sauce for serving

Instructions:

1. In a bowl, beat the eggs and season with salt and pepper.
2. Heat a non-stick skillet over medium heat and scramble the eggs until cooked through.
3. Warm the tortillas in the skillet for about 30 seconds on each side.
4. Divide the scrambled eggs between the tortillas.
5. Top with cherry tomatoes, feta cheese, Kalamata olives, and chopped spinach.
6. Roll the tortillas into burritos, securing them with toothpicks if needed.
7. Serve with a side of tzatziki sauce for a flavorful Greek-style breakfast!

Nutritional Values (per serving):

- Calories: 380
- Fat: 20g
- Carbs: 30g
- Protein: 20g

Orange and Almond Breakfast Couscous

Servings: 2
Prep Time: 10 minutes
Cook Time: 10 minutes
Ingredients:

- 1 cup whole wheat couscous
- 1 cup orange juice
- Zest of 1 orange
- 2 tablespoons honey
- 1/4 cup sliced almonds, toasted
- Fresh mint leaves for garnish

Instructions:

1. In a saucepan, bring the orange juice and zest to a boil.
2. Stir in the couscous, cover, and remove from heat. Let it sit for 5 minutes.
3. Fluff the couscous with a fork and drizzle honey over it, mixing well.
4. Toast the sliced almonds in a dry skillet until golden brown.
5. Sprinkle the toasted almonds over the couscous.
6. Garnish with fresh mint leaves for a burst of flavor and color.
7. Serve this delightful orange and almond breakfast couscous warm.

Nutritional Values (per serving):

- Calories: 380
- Fat: 8g
- Carbs: 70g
- Protein: 8g

Labneh and Cucumber Bagel

Servings: 1
Prep Time: 10 minutes
Ingredients:

- 1 whole wheat bagel
- 4 tablespoons labneh (strained yogurt)
- 1/2 cucumber, thinly sliced
- 1 tablespoon fresh dill, chopped
- Salt and pepper to taste

Instructions:

1. Slice the whole wheat bagel in half and toast it to your liking.
2. Spread a generous layer of labneh on each bagel half.
3. Arrange thinly sliced cucumber on top of the labneh.
4. Sprinkle fresh dill over the cucumber slices.
5. Season with salt and pepper to taste.
6. Assemble the bagel halves to form a delicious Labneh and Cucumber Bagel.

Nutritional Values (per serving):

- Calories: 320
- Fat: 8g

- Carbs: 50g
- Protein: 15g

Cherry Tomato and Basil Frittata

Servings: 4
Prep Time: 20 minutes
Cook Time: 10 minutes
Ingredients:
- 8 large eggs
- 1 cup cherry tomatoes, halved
- 1/4 cup fresh basil, chopped
- 1/2 cup feta cheese, crumbled
- Salt and pepper to taste
- 2 tablespoons olive oil

Instructions:
1. Preheat the broiler in your oven.
2. In a bowl, whisk together the eggs, cherry tomatoes, basil, and crumbled feta. Season with salt and pepper.
3. Heat olive oil in an oven-safe skillet over medium heat.
4. Pour the egg mixture into the skillet and let it cook without stirring for a few minutes until the edges set.
5. Transfer the skillet to the preheated broiler and cook for an additional 3-5 minutes until the top is golden and the center is set.
6. Remove from the oven, let it cool slightly, then slice into wedges.

Nutritional Values (per serving):
- Calories: 220
- Fat: 16g
- Carbs: 4g
- Protein: 14g

Almond Butter and Banana Smoothie Bowl

Servings: 2
Prep Time: 10 minutes
Ingredients:
- 2 ripe bananas, frozen
- 1/4 cup almond butter
- 1 cup Greek yogurt
- 1/2 cup almond milk
- 1 tablespoon honey
- Toppings: sliced almonds, chia seeds, banana slices

Instructions:
1. In a blender, combine frozen bananas, almond butter, Greek yogurt, almond milk, and honey.
2. Blend until smooth and creamy, adding more almond milk if needed.
3. Pour the smoothie into bowls.
4. Top with sliced almonds, chia seeds, and banana slices.
5. Serve immediately and enjoy!

Nutritional Values (per serving):
- Calories: 380
- Fat: 22g
- Carbs: 38g
- Protein: 15g

Mediterranean Breakfast Wrap

Servings: 1
Prep Time: 15 minutes
Ingredients:
- 1 whole wheat tortilla
- 2 large eggs, scrambled
- 1/4 cup diced tomatoes
- 2 tablespoons crumbled feta cheese
- 1 tablespoon chopped Kalamata olives
- 1 tablespoon chopped fresh parsley
- Salt and pepper to taste
- 1/4 cup baby spinach leaves

Instructions:
1. In a non-stick pan, scramble the eggs until fully cooked.
2. Place the whole wheat tortilla on a flat surface.
3. Spread the scrambled eggs over the center of the tortilla.

4. Top with diced tomatoes, feta cheese, Kalamata olives, chopped parsley, salt, and pepper.
5. Add baby spinach leaves on top.
6. Fold the sides of the tortilla and roll it into a wrap.
7. Heat the wrap in the pan for 1-2 minutes on each side until it's lightly toasted.
8. Serve warm and enjoy!

Nutritional Values:

- Calories: 380
- Fat: 18g
- Carbs: 32g
- Protein: 22g

SNACKS AND APPETIZER

Greek Spinach and Feta Stuffed Mushrooms

Servings: 4
Cooking Time: 20 minutes
Ingredients:

- 24 large mushrooms, stems removed and finely chopped
- 1 tablespoon olive oil
- 2 cups fresh spinach, chopped
- 1/2 cup crumbled feta cheese
- 2 cloves garlic, minced
- 1/4 cup breadcrumbs
- 1 teaspoon dried oregano
- Salt and pepper to taste
- Fresh parsley, chopped (for garnish)

Instructions:

1. Preheat the oven to 375°F (190°C).
2. In a pan, heat olive oil over medium heat. Add chopped mushroom stems and garlic, sauté until softened.
3. Add chopped spinach to the pan, cook until wilted. Season with salt and pepper.
4. In a bowl, combine the spinach mixture with feta, breadcrumbs, and dried oregano.
5. Place mushroom caps on a baking sheet. Stuff each cap with the spinach and feta mixture.
6. Bake for about 15 minutes or until mushrooms are tender.
7. Garnish with fresh parsley before serving.

Nutritional Values (per serving):

- Calories: 120
- Fat: 8g
- Carbs: 9g
- Protein: 5g

Hummus and Veggie Platter

Servings: 4
Preparation Time: 15 minutes
Ingredients:

- 1 cup hummus
- 2 carrots, sliced into sticks
- 1 cucumber, sliced
- 1 bell pepper (assorted colors), sliced
- Cherry tomatoes
- Kalamata olives
- Whole grain pita bread, cut into triangles

Instructions:

1. Arrange a generous scoop of hummus in the center of a serving platter.

2. Surround the hummus with carrot sticks, cucumber slices, bell pepper strips, cherry tomatoes, and Kalamata olives.
3. Place the pita triangles around the edge of the platter.
4. Serve immediately and enjoy the variety of flavors and textures.

Nutritional Values (per serving):
- Calories: 180
- Fat: 8g
- Carbs: 24g
- Protein: 6g

Mediterranean Bruschetta with Tomato and Olive Tapenade

Servings: 6
Preparation Time: 20 minutes

Ingredients:
- 1 baguette, sliced
- 2 cups cherry tomatoes, diced
- 1/2 cup Kalamata olives, chopped
- 1/4 cup red onion, finely diced
- 2 cloves garlic, minced
- 2 tablespoons extra-virgin olive oil
- 1 tablespoon balsamic vinegar
- Fresh basil leaves for garnish
- Salt and pepper to taste

Instructions:
1. Preheat the oven broiler. Place the baguette slices on a baking sheet and toast until golden brown.
2. In a bowl, combine cherry tomatoes, Kalamata olives, red onion, garlic, olive oil, and balsamic vinegar. Mix well.
3. Spoon the tomato and olive tapenade over the toasted baguette slices.
4. Garnish with fresh basil leaves and season with salt and pepper to taste.
5. Serve as a delightful Mediterranean-inspired appetizer.

Nutritional Values (per serving):
- Calories: 150
- Fat: 7g
- Carbs: 18g
- Protein: 3g

Baked Falafel Bites with Tahini Sauce

Servings: 4
Preparation Time: 25 minutes
Ingredients:
- 1 can (15 oz) chickpeas, drained and rinsed
- 1/4 cup fresh parsley, chopped
- 1/4 cup red onion, finely chopped
- 2 cloves garlic, minced
- 1 teaspoon ground cumin
- 1 teaspoon ground coriander
- 1/2 teaspoon baking powder
- Salt and pepper to taste
- Olive oil cooking spray
- Tahini sauce for dipping

Instructions:
1. Preheat the oven to 375°F (190°C).
2. In a food processor, combine chickpeas, parsley, red onion, garlic, cumin, coriander, baking powder, salt, and pepper. Pulse until well combined.
3. Shape the mixture into small falafel bites and place them on a baking sheet lined with parchment paper.
4. Lightly spray the falafel bites with olive oil cooking spray.
5. Bake for 20 minutes or until golden brown, turning halfway through.
6. Serve the baked falafel bites with a side of tahini sauce for a delicious and nutritious snack.

Nutritional Values (per serving):
- Calories: 180
- Fat: 8g
- Carbs: 22g
- Protein: 7g

Marinated Artichoke Hearts with Lemon and Herbs

Servings: 6
Preparation Time: 15 minutes
Ingredients:

- 1 jar (12 oz) marinated artichoke hearts, drained
- Zest of 1 lemon
- 2 tablespoons fresh parsley, finely chopped
- 1 tablespoon fresh dill, finely chopped
- 1 clove garlic, minced
- 2 tablespoons extra-virgin olive oil
- Salt and pepper to taste

Instructions:

1. In a bowl, combine the drained artichoke hearts, lemon zest, chopped parsley, chopped dill, and minced garlic.
2. Drizzle extra-virgin olive oil over the mixture and toss until the artichoke hearts are well coated.
3. Season with salt and pepper to taste. Adjust the seasonings if needed.
4. Allow the artichoke hearts to marinate for at least 10 minutes to let the flavors meld.
5. Serve as a refreshing and flavorful appetizer or snack.

Nutritional Values (per serving):

- Calories: 90
- Fat: 7g
- Carbs: 5g
- Protein: 2g

Olive and Herb Focaccia Bread

Servings: 8
Preparation Time: 25 minutes (plus rising time)
Ingredients:

- 2 1/4 teaspoons (1 packet) active dry yeast
- 1 teaspoon sugar
- 1 cup warm water (110°F/43°C)
- 3 cups all-purpose flour
- 1 teaspoon salt
- 1/3 cup extra-virgin olive oil
- 1/2 cup Kalamata olives, pitted and halved
- 2 tablespoons fresh rosemary, chopped
- Coarse sea salt for sprinkling

Instructions:

1. In a small bowl, combine the active dry yeast, sugar, and warm water. Let it sit for about 5 minutes until foamy.
2. In a large mixing bowl, combine the flour and salt. Make a well in the center and pour in the yeast mixture and olive oil. Mix until a dough forms.
3. Knead the dough on a floured surface for about 5 minutes until smooth. Place the dough in a greased bowl, cover with a damp cloth, and let it rise in a warm place for 1 hour.
4. Preheat the oven to 425°F (220°C). Punch down the dough and roll it out into a rectangle on a baking sheet.
5. Press olives into the dough, sprinkle with chopped rosemary, and drizzle with olive oil. Let it rest for 15 minutes.
6. Bake for 15-20 minutes or until golden brown. Sprinkle with coarse sea salt.
7. Slice and serve this savory and aromatic focaccia as an appetizer or snack.

Nutritional Values (per serving):

- Calories: 260
- Fat: 10g
- Carbs: 35g
- Protein: 5g

Tzatziki Cucumber Cups

Servings: 12
Preparation Time: 15 minutes
Ingredients:

- 2 large cucumbers
- 1 cup Greek yogurt
- 1/2 cup cucumber, finely diced
- 1 clove garlic, minced
- 1 tablespoon fresh dill, chopped
- 1 tablespoon extra-virgin olive oil
- 1 tablespoon lemon juice

- Salt and pepper to taste
- Cherry tomatoes and fresh dill for garnish

Instructions:

1. Peel the cucumbers and slice them into 1-inch thick rounds. Use a melon baller or a teaspoon to scoop out the center, creating a cup.
2. In a bowl, combine Greek yogurt, diced cucumber, minced garlic, chopped dill, olive oil, and lemon juice. Mix well.
3. Season the mixture with salt and pepper to taste. Stir until all ingredients are evenly incorporated.
4. Spoon the tzatziki mixture into the cucumber cups.
5. Garnish each cup with a halved cherry tomato and a small sprig of fresh dill.
6. Arrange the cucumber cups on a serving platter and refrigerate until ready to serve.

These refreshing Tzatziki Cucumber Cups make a delightful Mediterranean-inspired snack or appetizer.

Nutritional Values (per serving):
- Calories: 45
- Fat: 3g
- Carbs: 3g
- Protein: 2g

Roasted Red Pepper and Feta Dip

Servings: 8
Preparation Time: 20 minutes
Ingredients:
- 1 cup roasted red peppers, drained and chopped
- 1/2 cup crumbled feta cheese
- 1/4 cup Greek yogurt
- 2 tablespoons extra-virgin olive oil
- 1 clove garlic, minced
- 1 teaspoon lemon juice
- 1/2 teaspoon dried oregano
- Salt and pepper to taste
- Fresh parsley for garnish

Instructions:

1. In a food processor, combine roasted red peppers, feta cheese, Greek yogurt, olive oil, minced garlic, lemon juice, and dried oregano.
2. Pulse the ingredients until the mixture reaches a smooth and creamy consistency.
3. Season the dip with salt and pepper to taste. Blend again to incorporate the seasoning.
4. Transfer the dip to a serving bowl and garnish with fresh parsley.
5. Serve with pita chips, sliced cucumbers, or carrot sticks.

This Roasted Red Pepper and Feta Dip is a flavorful and vibrant addition to your Mediterranean snack repertoire.

Nutritional Values (per serving):
- Calories: 80
- Fat: 6g
- Carbs: 4g
- Protein: 3g

Greek Salad Skewers

Servings: 6
Preparation Time: 15 minutes
Ingredients:
- 1 cup cherry tomatoes
- 1 cucumber, cut into chunks
- 1 cup Kalamata olives, pitted
- 1 cup feta cheese, cubed
- 1/2 red onion, cut into wedges
- 2 tablespoons extra-virgin olive oil
- 1 tablespoon red wine vinegar
- 1 teaspoon dried oregano
- Salt and pepper to taste
- Wooden skewers

Instructions:

1. Thread cherry tomatoes, cucumber chunks, Kalamata olives, feta cheese cubes, and red onion wedges onto wooden skewers in a colorful and appealing pattern.
2. In a small bowl, whisk together extra-virgin olive oil, red wine vinegar, dried oregano, salt, and pepper to create the dressing.

3. Drizzle the dressing over the assembled skewers, ensuring each piece is coated with the flavorful dressing.
4. Arrange the Greek Salad Skewers on a serving platter and refrigerate until ready to serve.
5. Serve chilled as a delightful and refreshing Mediterranean appetizer.

Nutritional Values (per serving):
- Calories: 120
- Fat: 10g
- Carbs: 5g
- Protein: 4g

Zucchini Fritters with Yogurt Sauce

Servings: 4
Preparation Time: 25 minutes
Ingredients:
- 2 medium zucchinis, grated
- 1 teaspoon salt
- 1/2 cup feta cheese, crumbled
- 1/4 cup fresh mint, finely chopped
- 1/4 cup fresh dill, finely chopped
- 1/4 cup green onions, finely sliced
- 1/2 cup breadcrumbs
- 1 large egg, beaten
- 2 tablespoons olive oil
- 1 cup Greek yogurt
- 1 tablespoon lemon juice
- 1 clove garlic, minced
- Salt and pepper to taste

Instructions:
1. Place the grated zucchini in a colander, sprinkle with salt, and let it sit for 10 minutes. Squeeze out excess moisture using a clean kitchen towel.
2. In a large bowl, combine the grated zucchini, feta cheese, mint, dill, green onions, breadcrumbs, and beaten egg. Mix until well combined.
3. Form the mixture into small patties and set aside.

4. Heat olive oil in a skillet over medium heat. Cook the zucchini fritters for 3-4 minutes on each side or until golden brown.
5. In a small bowl, mix Greek yogurt, lemon juice, minced garlic, salt, and pepper to prepare the yogurt sauce.
6. Serve the zucchini fritters with a dollop of yogurt sauce on top.

Nutritional Values (per serving):
- Calories: 220
- Fat: 12g
- Carbs: 18g
- Protein: 9g

Stuffed Grape Leaves (Dolma) with Tzatziki

Servings: 6
Preparation Time: 30 minutes
Ingredients: *For Dolma:*
- 1 cup grape leaves, preserved in brine, drained
- 1 cup cooked long-grain rice
- 1/2 cup pine nuts, toasted
- 1/4 cup fresh parsley, chopped
- 1/4 cup fresh dill, chopped
- 1/4 cup raisins, chopped
- 1 teaspoon ground cinnamon
- 1/2 teaspoon ground allspice
- Salt and pepper to taste
- 2 tablespoons olive oil
- 1 lemon, juiced

For Tzatziki:
- 1 cup Greek yogurt
- 1/2 cucumber, finely diced
- 2 tablespoons fresh mint, chopped
- 1 clove garlic, minced
- 1 tablespoon olive oil
- Salt and pepper to taste

Instructions:
1. In a bowl, combine cooked rice, pine nuts, parsley, dill, raisins, cinnamon, allspice, salt, and pepper to make the dolma filling.

2. Place a grape leaf on a flat surface, shiny side down. Trim the stem and place a spoonful of filling in the center.
3. Fold the sides of the grape leaf over the filling and roll tightly from the bottom to the top.
4. Repeat with the remaining grape leaves and filling.
5. Arrange the stuffed grape leaves in a serving dish.

For Tzatziki:

1. In a separate bowl, mix Greek yogurt, cucumber, mint, garlic, olive oil, salt, and pepper to prepare the tzatziki sauce.
2. Serve the stuffed grape leaves with a side of tzatziki sauce.

Nutritional Values (per serving):
- Calories: 220
- Fat: 12g
- Carbs: 25g
- Protein: 7g

Caprese Salad Skewers with Balsamic Glaze

Servings: 4
Preparation Time: 20 minutes
Ingredients:
- 1 pint cherry tomatoes
- 8 ounces fresh mozzarella balls
- Fresh basil leaves
- Balsamic glaze
- Salt and pepper to taste
- Wooden skewers

Instructions:
1. Thread a cherry tomato onto a skewer, followed by a mozzarella ball and a fresh basil leaf. Repeat until the skewer is filled.
2. Arrange the skewers on a serving platter.
3. Drizzle balsamic glaze over the skewers.
4. Sprinkle with salt and pepper to taste.

Nutritional Values (per serving):
- Calories: 150
- Fat: 10g

- Carbs: 8g
- Protein: 8g

Pistachio and Herb-Crusted Goat Cheese Balls

Servings:4
Cooking Time: 15 minutes
Ingredients:
- 8 oz goat cheese, softened
- 1/2 cup shelled pistachios, finely chopped
- 2 tablespoons fresh parsley, finely chopped
- 1 tablespoon fresh chives, finely chopped
- 1 tablespoon honey
- Crackers, for serving

Instructions:
1. In a bowl, mix the softened goat cheese, chopped pistachios, parsley, and chives until well combined.
2. Scoop small portions of the mixture and roll them into bite-sized balls.
3. Place the goat cheese balls on a plate and refrigerate for 10 minutes to firm up.
4. Drizzle honey over the chilled goat cheese balls just before serving.
5. Serve with your favorite crackers.

Nutritional Values (per serving):
- Calories: 250
- Fat: 18g
- Carbs: 10g
- Protein: 12g

Spanakopita Triangles

Servings:6
Cooking Time: 25 minutes
Ingredients:
- 8 oz frozen spinach, thawed and drained
- 4 oz feta cheese, crumbled
- 1/2 cup ricotta cheese
- 1/4 cup fresh dill, chopped
- 2 green onions, finely chopped
- 1 egg, beaten

- 1 package phyllo dough, thawed
- 1/4 cup olive oil, for brushing

Instructions:
1. Preheat the oven to 375°F (190°C).
2. In a bowl, combine the thawed and drained spinach, feta cheese, ricotta cheese, dill, green onions, and beaten egg. Mix well.
3. Lay out one sheet of phyllo dough and brush it lightly with olive oil. Place another sheet on top and repeat until you have three layers.
4. Cut the phyllo dough into strips. Spoon a small amount of the spinach mixture onto one end of each strip and fold into a triangle shape.
5. Place the triangles on a baking sheet and brush the tops with olive oil.
6. Bake for 15-18 minutes or until golden brown.
7. Allow to cool slightly before serving.

Nutritional Values (per serving):
- Calories: 280
- Fat: 18g
- Carbs: 22g
- Protein: 8g

Roasted Garlic and White Bean Dip

Servings:4
Cooking Time: 20 minutes
Ingredients:
- 15 oz can white beans, drained and rinsed
- 1 head of garlic
- 2 tbsp olive oil
- 1 tbsp lemon juice
- 1 tsp cumin
- Salt and pepper to taste
- Fresh parsley for garnish

Instructions:
1. Preheat the oven to 400°F (200°C).
2. Cut the top off the head of garlic, exposing the cloves. Drizzle with olive oil, wrap in foil, and roast for 15-20 minutes or until garlic is soft.
3. In a food processor, combine the white beans, roasted garlic cloves (squeeze them out of the skin), olive oil, lemon juice, cumin, salt, and pepper. Blend until smooth.
4. Adjust seasoning to taste.
5. Transfer the dip to a serving bowl, drizzle with a bit of olive oil, and garnish with fresh parsley.
6. Serve with pita chips or vegetable sticks.

Nutritional Values (per serving):
- Calories: 180
- Fat: 7g
- Carbs: 23g
- Protein: 7g

SALADS

Mediterranean Quinoa Salad with Chickpeas

Servings: 4
Cooking Time: 20 minutes
Ingredients:
- 1 cup quinoa, rinsed
- 2 cups water
- 1 can (15 oz) chickpeas, drained and rinsed
- 1 cup cherry tomatoes, halved
- 1 cucumber, diced
- 1/2 red onion, finely chopped
- 1/2 cup Kalamata olives, sliced
- 1/2 cup crumbled feta cheese
- 1/4 cup fresh parsley, chopped
- 1/4 cup extra-virgin olive oil

- 2 tablespoons red wine vinegar
- 1 teaspoon dried oregano
- Salt and pepper to taste

Instructions:
1. In a medium saucepan, combine quinoa and water. Bring to a boil, then reduce heat, cover, and simmer for 15 minutes, or until quinoa is cooked and water is absorbed. Fluff with a fork and let it cool.
2. In a large bowl, combine cooked quinoa, chickpeas, cherry tomatoes, cucumber, red onion, olives, feta cheese, and parsley.
3. In a small bowl, whisk together olive oil, red wine vinegar, dried oregano, salt, and pepper to create the dressing.
4. Pour the dressing over the quinoa mixture and toss until well combined.
5. Serve immediately or refrigerate until ready to serve. Enjoy this refreshing and nutrient-packed Mediterranean quinoa salad!

Nutritional Values (per serving):
- Calories: 380
- Fat: 20g
- Carbs: 40g
- Protein: 12g

Roasted Red Pepper and Feta Pasta Salad

Servings: 6
Cooking Time: 25 minutes
Ingredients:
- 8 oz whole wheat pasta
- 1 cup roasted red peppers, sliced
- 1/2 cup crumbled feta cheese
- 1/4 cup Kalamata olives, chopped
- 1/4 cup fresh basil, chopped
- 2 tablespoons extra-virgin olive oil
- 1 tablespoon balsamic vinegar
- 1 clove garlic, minced
- Salt and pepper to taste

Instructions:
1. Cook the whole wheat pasta according to package instructions. Drain and let it cool.
2. In a large bowl, combine cooked pasta, roasted red peppers, feta cheese, olives, and fresh basil.
3. In a small bowl, whisk together olive oil, balsamic vinegar, minced garlic, salt, and pepper to create the dressing.
4. Pour the dressing over the pasta mixture and toss until well coated.
5. Serve chilled or at room temperature. This Roasted Red Pepper and Feta Pasta Salad are a delightful addition to your Mediterranean feast!

Nutritional Values (per serving):
- Calories: 280
- Fat: 10g
- Carbs: 38g
- Protein: 8g

Lemon Herb Couscous Salad

Servings: 4
Cooking Time: 20 minutes
Ingredients:
- 1 cup whole wheat couscous
- 1 1/2 cups vegetable broth
- Zest and juice of 1 lemon
- 2 tablespoons extra-virgin olive oil
- 1/4 cup fresh parsley, chopped
- 1/4 cup fresh mint, chopped
- 1 cucumber, diced
- 1 cup cherry tomatoes, halved
- Salt and pepper to taste

Instructions:
1. In a saucepan, bring the vegetable broth to a boil. Stir in the couscous, cover, and remove from heat. Let it sit for 5 minutes, then fluff with a fork.
2. In a large bowl, combine the cooked couscous, lemon zest, lemon juice, olive oil, parsley, mint, cucumber, and cherry tomatoes.
3. Gently toss the ingredients until well mixed. Season with salt and pepper to taste.

4. Chill the salad in the refrigerator for at least 15 minutes before serving.
5. Enjoy this refreshing Lemon Herb Couscous Salad as a light and zesty side dish in your Mediterranean spread!

Nutritional Values (per serving):
- Calories: 220
- Fat: 7g
- Carbs: 35g
- Protein: 5g

Greek Cucumber and Tomato Salad

Servings: 4
Cooking Time: 15 minutes
Ingredients:
- 2 large cucumbers, diced
- 2 cups cherry tomatoes, halved
- 1 red onion, thinly sliced
- 1/2 cup Kalamata olives, pitted and sliced
- 1/2 cup crumbled feta cheese
- 1/4 cup extra-virgin olive oil
- 2 tablespoons red wine vinegar
- 1 teaspoon dried oregano
- Salt and pepper to taste
- Fresh parsley for garnish

Instructions:
1. In a large bowl, combine the diced cucumbers, cherry tomatoes, red onion, olives, and feta cheese.
2. In a small bowl, whisk together the olive oil, red wine vinegar, dried oregano, salt, and pepper to create the dressing.
3. Pour the dressing over the salad and toss gently to coat the ingredients evenly.
4. Garnish with fresh parsley and let the flavors meld for about 10 minutes.
5. Serve this Greek Cucumber and Tomato Salad as a vibrant and nutritious side dish in your Mediterranean feast!

Nutritional Values (per serving):
- Calories: 210
- Fat: 16g

- Carbs: 14g
- Protein: 6g

Spinach and Strawberry Salad with Balsamic Vinaigrette

Servings: 4
Cooking Time: 10 minutes
Ingredients:
- 6 cups fresh baby spinach
- 1 pint strawberries, hulled and sliced
- 1/2 cup sliced almonds, toasted
- 1/4 cup crumbled goat cheese
- 2 tablespoons balsamic vinegar
- 1 tablespoon extra-virgin olive oil
- 1 teaspoon honey
- Salt and pepper to taste

Instructions:
1. In a large salad bowl, combine the fresh baby spinach, sliced strawberries, toasted almonds, and crumbled goat cheese.
2. In a small bowl, whisk together the balsamic vinegar, olive oil, honey, salt, and pepper to create the vinaigrette.
3. Drizzle the balsamic vinaigrette over the salad and toss gently to coat the ingredients evenly.
4. Serve this refreshing Spinach and Strawberry Salad as a delightful side with a perfect balance of sweet and savory flavors.

Nutritional Values (per serving):
- Calories: 180
- Fat: 12g
- Carbs: 15g
- Protein: 5g

Italian Farro Salad with Sun-Dried Tomatoes

Servings: 6
Cooking Time: 25 minutes
Ingredients:
- 1 cup farro

- 2 cups water
- 1/2 cup sun-dried tomatoes, chopped
- 1/3 cup Kalamata olives, sliced
- 1/4 cup red onion, finely chopped
- 1/4 cup fresh parsley, chopped
- 1/4 cup feta cheese, crumbled
- 2 tablespoons extra-virgin olive oil
- 1 tablespoon red wine vinegar
- Salt and pepper to taste

Instructions:

1. Rinse the farro under cold water. In a saucepan, combine the rinsed farro and water. Bring to a boil, then reduce heat, cover, and simmer for 20-25 minutes or until the farro is tender but still chewy. Drain any excess water.
2. In a large bowl, combine the cooked farro, sun-dried tomatoes, Kalamata olives, red onion, parsley, and feta cheese.
3. In a small bowl, whisk together the olive oil, red wine vinegar, salt, and pepper. Pour the dressing over the salad and toss to combine.
4. Serve this Italian Farro Salad as a satisfying side dish or a light lunch.

Nutritional Values (per serving):

- Calories: 220
- Fat: 8g
- Carbs: 32g
- Protein: 6g

Mediterranean Lentil Salad with Feta

Servings: 4
Cooking Time: 30 minutes
Ingredients:

- 1 cup green lentils, rinsed
- 3 cups water
- 1 cucumber, diced
- 1 cup cherry tomatoes, halved
- 1/2 cup red bell pepper, diced
- 1/4 cup red onion, finely chopped
- 1/3 cup crumbled feta cheese
- 2 tablespoons fresh parsley, chopped

- 3 tablespoons extra-virgin olive oil
- 2 tablespoons red wine vinegar
- 1 teaspoon dried oregano
- Salt and pepper to taste

Instructions:

1. In a medium saucepan, combine the rinsed lentils and water. Bring to a boil, then reduce heat, cover, and simmer for 20-25 minutes or until lentils are tender but still hold their shape. Drain any excess water.
2. In a large bowl, combine the cooked lentils, cucumber, cherry tomatoes, red bell pepper, red onion, feta cheese, and fresh parsley.
3. In a small bowl, whisk together the olive oil, red wine vinegar, dried oregano, salt, and pepper. Pour the dressing over the salad and toss to combine.
4. Allow the flavors to meld for a few minutes before serving. This lentil salad is delightful as a light lunch or a refreshing side dish.

Nutritional Values (per serving):

- Calories: 320
- Fat: 14g
- Carbs: 36g
- Protein: 15g

Artichoke, Olive, and Feta Greek Salad

Servings: 4
Cooking Time: 20 minutes
Ingredients:

- 2 cups cherry tomatoes, halved
- 1 cucumber, diced
- 1 can (14 oz) artichoke hearts, drained and quartered
- 1/2 cup Kalamata olives, pitted
- 1/3 cup crumbled feta cheese
- 1/4 cup red onion, thinly sliced
- 2 tablespoons fresh oregano, chopped
- 3 tablespoons extra-virgin olive oil
- 2 tablespoons red wine vinegar
- Salt and pepper to taste

Instructions:

1. In a large bowl, combine cherry tomatoes, cucumber, artichoke hearts, Kalamata olives, feta cheese, red onion, and fresh oregano.
2. In a small bowl, whisk together olive oil, red wine vinegar, salt, and pepper.
3. Pour the dressing over the salad and toss gently to coat all ingredients.
4. Allow the salad to marinate for at least 10 minutes before serving to enhance the flavors.
5. Serve this vibrant Greek salad as a refreshing side dish or a light, wholesome lunch option.

Nutritional Values (per serving):

- Calories: 240
- Fat: 18g
- Carbs: 15g
- Protein: 6g

Bulgur and Vegetable Salad with Lemon Dressing
Servings: 4
Cooking Time: 25 minutes
Ingredients:

- 1 cup fine bulgur
- 1 1/2 cups boiling water
- 1 cup cherry tomatoes, halved
- 1 bell pepper, diced
- 1 cucumber, peeled and diced
- 1/4 cup red onion, finely chopped
- 1/4 cup fresh parsley, chopped
- Zest of 1 lemon
- 3 tablespoons lemon juice
- 3 tablespoons extra-virgin olive oil
- Salt and pepper to taste

Instructions:

1. Place the bulgur in a bowl and pour boiling water over it. Cover and let it sit for 15 minutes or until the water is absorbed.
2. Fluff the bulgur with a fork and let it cool to room temperature.
3. In a large bowl, combine the cooled bulgur, cherry tomatoes, bell pepper, cucumber, red onion, and fresh parsley.

4. In a small bowl, whisk together lemon zest, lemon juice, olive oil, salt, and pepper.
5. Pour the lemon dressing over the salad and toss to combine.
6. Refrigerate the salad for at least 10 minutes before serving.
7. Enjoy this refreshing and nutritious Bulgur and Vegetable Salad as a side or a light main dish.

Nutritional Values (per serving):

- Calories: 210
- Fat: 10g
- Carbs: 28g
- Protein: 5g

Grilled Halloumi Salad with Fresh Herbs

Servings: 2
Cooking Time: 15 minutes
Ingredients:

- 8 oz halloumi cheese, sliced
- 2 cups mixed salad greens
- 1 cup cherry tomatoes, halved
- 1/2 cucumber, sliced
- 1/4 cup Kalamata olives, pitted
- 2 tablespoons fresh mint, chopped
- 2 tablespoons fresh basil, chopped
- 2 tablespoons extra-virgin olive oil
- 1 tablespoon balsamic vinegar
- Salt and pepper to taste

Instructions:

1. Heat a grill pan over medium-high heat. Grill the halloumi slices for 1-2 minutes per side or until golden brown grill marks appear.
2. In a large salad bowl, combine the mixed greens, cherry tomatoes, cucumber, olives, mint, and basil.
3. Arrange the grilled halloumi slices on top of the salad.
4. In a small bowl, whisk together olive oil, balsamic vinegar, salt, and pepper to create the dressing.

5. Drizzle the dressing over the salad and halloumi.
6. Gently toss the salad to combine all ingredients.
7. Serve immediately as a light and flavorful Grilled Halloumi Salad.

Nutritional Values (per serving):
- Calories: 380
- Fat: 32g
- Carbs: 10g
- Protein: 15g

Pomegranate and Walnut Spinach Salad

Servings: 4
Cooking Time: 15 minutes
Ingredients:
- 6 cups baby spinach leaves
- 1 cup pomegranate arils
- 1/2 cup walnuts, chopped
- 1/4 cup feta cheese, crumbled
- 2 tablespoons balsamic vinegar
- 2 tablespoons extra-virgin olive oil
- 1 tablespoon honey
- Salt and pepper to taste

Instructions:
1. In a large salad bowl, combine the baby spinach, pomegranate arils, walnuts, and feta cheese.
2. In a small bowl, whisk together balsamic vinegar, olive oil, honey, salt, and pepper to create the dressing.
3. Drizzle the dressing over the salad ingredients.
4. Gently toss the salad until well coated in the dressing.
5. Allow the salad to sit for a few minutes to let the flavors meld.
6. Serve the Pomegranate and Walnut Spinach Salad as a refreshing side or a light main dish.

Nutritional Values (per serving):
- Calories: 220

- Fat: 18g
- Carbs: 15g
- Protein: 5g

White Bean and Tuna Salad with Lemon-Oregano Dressing

Servings: 4
Cooking Time: 15 minutes
Ingredients:
- 2 cans (15 oz each) white beans, drained and rinsed
- 1 can (5 oz) tuna in olive oil, drained
- 1 cup cherry tomatoes, halved
- 1/2 red onion, finely chopped
- 1/4 cup Kalamata olives, sliced
- 2 tablespoons fresh parsley, chopped
- 2 tablespoons extra-virgin olive oil
- 1 tablespoon lemon juice
- 1 teaspoon dried oregano
- Salt and pepper to taste

Instructions:
1. In a large mixing bowl, combine white beans, tuna, cherry tomatoes, red onion, olives, and parsley.
2. In a small bowl, whisk together olive oil, lemon juice, dried oregano, salt, and pepper to create the dressing.
3. Pour the dressing over the salad ingredients.
4. Gently toss the salad until well combined.
5. Adjust salt and pepper according to taste.
6. Serve the White Bean and Tuna Salad as a protein-packed and flavorful salad.

Nutritional Values (per serving):
- Calories: 380
- Fat: 16g
- Carbs: 42g
- Protein: 22g

Israeli Salad with Radishes and Cucumber

Servings: 4

Cooking Time: 15 minutes

Ingredients:

- 4 medium-sized tomatoes, diced
- 2 cucumbers, diced
- 4 radishes, thinly sliced
- 1/2 red onion, finely chopped
- 1/4 cup fresh parsley, chopped
- 2 tablespoons extra-virgin olive oil
- 1 tablespoon red wine vinegar
- Salt and pepper to taste

Instructions:

1. In a large bowl, combine diced tomatoes, cucumbers, radishes, red onion, and fresh parsley.
2. In a small bowl, whisk together olive oil, red wine vinegar, salt, and pepper to create the dressing.
3. Pour the dressing over the salad ingredients.
4. Gently toss the salad until well combined.
5. Adjust salt and pepper according to taste.
6. Allow the salad to marinate for a few minutes before serving.
7. Serve the Israeli Salad with Radishes and Cucumber as a refreshing and vibrant side dish.

Nutritional Values (per serving):

- Calories: 110
- Fat: 7g
- Carbs: 12g
- Protein: 2g

Mediterranean Chickpea and Artichoke Salad

Servings: 4

Cooking Time: 20 minutes

Ingredients:

- 2 cans (15 oz each) chickpeas, drained and rinsed
- 1 can (14 oz) artichoke hearts, drained and chopped
- 1 cup cherry tomatoes, halved

- 1/2 red onion, finely chopped
- 1/4 cup Kalamata olives, sliced
- 1/4 cup fresh parsley, chopped
- 2 tablespoons feta cheese, crumbled
- 3 tablespoons extra-virgin olive oil
- 1 tablespoon balsamic vinegar
- Salt and pepper to taste

Instructions:

1. In a large bowl, combine chickpeas, chopped artichoke hearts, cherry tomatoes, red onion, olives, and fresh parsley.
2. In a small bowl, whisk together olive oil, balsamic vinegar, salt, and pepper to create the dressing.
3. Pour the dressing over the salad ingredients.
4. Gently toss the salad until well combined.
5. Sprinkle crumbled feta cheese on top.
6. Adjust salt and pepper according to taste.
7. Allow the salad to marinate for a few minutes before serving.
8. Serve the Mediterranean Chickpea and Artichoke Salad as a flavorful and protein-packed dish.

Nutritional Values (per serving):

- Calories: 320
- Fat: 18g
- Carbs: 34g
- Protein: 10g

Orzo Pasta Salad with Mediterranean Vegetables

Servings: 6

Cooking Time: 25 minutes

Ingredients:

- 1 cup orzo pasta
- 1 cup cherry tomatoes, halved
- 1 cucumber, diced
- 1/2 cup red bell pepper, chopped
- 1/4 cup red onion, finely chopped
- 1/4 cup Kalamata olives, sliced
- 1/4 cup crumbled feta cheese
- 2 tablespoons fresh basil, chopped

- 3 tablespoons extra-virgin olive oil
- 2 tablespoons balsamic vinegar
- Salt and pepper to taste

Instructions:

1. Cook orzo pasta according to package instructions. Drain and let it cool.
2. In a large bowl, combine cooked orzo, cherry tomatoes, cucumber, red bell pepper, red onion, olives, and feta cheese.
3. In a small bowl, whisk together olive oil, balsamic vinegar, salt, and pepper to create the dressing.
4. Pour the dressing over the pasta and vegetables.
5. Gently toss the salad until well coated.
6. Sprinkle fresh basil on top for added flavor.
7. Adjust salt and pepper according to taste.
8. Refrigerate for at least 15 minutes before serving.
9. Present the Orzo Pasta Salad with Mediterranean Vegetables as a delightful side dish or a light lunch option.

Nutritional Values (per serving):

- Calories: 280
- Fat: 12g
- Carbs: 38g
- Protein: 7g

BEANS GRAINS AND RICE

Mediterranean Chickpea Salad

Servings: 4
Cooking Time: 20 minutes
Ingredients:

- 1 can (15 oz) chickpeas, drained and rinsed
- 1 cup cherry tomatoes, halved
- 1 cucumber, diced
- 1/2 red onion, finely chopped
- 1/4 cup Kalamata olives, sliced
- 1/4 cup crumbled feta cheese
- 2 tablespoons extra-virgin olive oil
- 1 tablespoon red wine vinegar
- 1 teaspoon dried oregano
- Salt and pepper to taste
- Fresh parsley for garnish

Instructions:

1. In a large bowl, combine chickpeas, cherry tomatoes, cucumber, red onion, olives, and feta cheese.
2. In a small bowl, whisk together olive oil, red wine vinegar, dried oregano, salt, and pepper.
3. Pour the dressing over the salad and toss to coat evenly.
4. Allow the salad to marinate for at least 10 minutes to enhance flavors.
5. Garnish with fresh parsley before serving.

Nutritional Values (per serving):

- Calories: 280
- Fat: 14g
- Carbs: 30g
- Protein: 9g

Lemon Garlic Herb Quinoa

Servings: 4
Cooking Time: 15 minutes
Ingredients:

- 1 cup quinoa
- 2 cups vegetable broth
- Zest and juice of 1 lemon
- 2 cloves garlic, minced
- 2 tablespoons fresh parsley, chopped
- 1 tablespoon fresh thyme leaves
- Salt and pepper to taste
- 2 tablespoons extra-virgin olive oil

Instructions:

1. Rinse quinoa under cold water. In a saucepan, combine quinoa and vegetable broth.
2. Bring to a boil, then reduce heat, cover, and simmer for 12-15 minutes or until quinoa is cooked and liquid is absorbed.
3. Fluff the quinoa with a fork and transfer to a large bowl.
4. In a small bowl, whisk together lemon zest, lemon juice, minced garlic, parsley, thyme, salt, and pepper.
5. Pour the herb mixture over the quinoa and toss to combine.
6. Drizzle with olive oil and toss again before serving.

Nutritional Values (per serving):

- Calories: 220
- Fat: 7g
- Carbs: 32g
- Protein: 6g

Tomato and Basil Farro Risotto

Servings: 4
Cooking Time: 25 minutes
Ingredients:

- 1 cup farro
- 4 cups vegetable broth
- 1 tablespoon olive oil
- 1 onion, finely chopped
- 2 cloves garlic, minced
- 1 cup cherry tomatoes, halved

- 1/4 cup fresh basil, chopped
- Salt and pepper to taste
- 1/2 cup grated Parmesan cheese (optional)

Instructions:
1. In a saucepan, bring the vegetable broth to a simmer and keep it warm.
2. In a separate large pan, heat olive oil over medium heat. Add chopped onions and garlic, sauté until softened.
3. Add farro to the pan, stirring to coat with the oil, for 1-2 minutes.
4. Begin adding the warm broth, one ladle at a time, allowing the liquid to be absorbed before adding more. Continue until farro is tender.
5. Stir in cherry tomatoes and fresh basil. Cook for an additional 2-3 minutes.
6. Season with salt and pepper. If desired, stir in Parmesan cheese.
7. Serve warm and enjoy!

Nutritional Values (per serving):
- Calories: 280
- Fat: 5g
- Carbs: 50g
- Protein: 9g

Greek Lentil Soup with Spinach

Servings: 6
Cooking Time: 30 minutes
Ingredients:
- 1 cup dried green lentils
- 1 onion, diced
- 2 carrots, sliced
- 2 celery stalks, chopped
- 3 cloves garlic, minced
- 1 can (14 oz) diced tomatoes
- 1 teaspoon dried oregano
- 1 teaspoon ground cumin
- 1/2 teaspoon smoked paprika
- 6 cups vegetable broth
- 4 cups fresh spinach
- Salt and pepper to taste
- Lemon wedges for serving

Instructions:
1. Rinse lentils under cold water and set aside.
2. In a large pot, sauté onions, carrots, and celery until softened.
3. Add garlic, oregano, cumin, and smoked paprika. Stir for 1-2 minutes.
4. Pour in the vegetable broth and add lentils. Bring to a boil, then reduce heat and simmer for 20-25 minutes.
5. Add diced tomatoes with their juice and continue to simmer for an additional 5 minutes.
6. Stir in fresh spinach until wilted. Season with salt and pepper.
7. Serve hot, with a squeeze of fresh lemon juice.

Nutritional Values (per serving):
- Calories: 220
- Fat: 1.5g
- Carbs: 40g
- Protein: 13g

Spinach and Feta Stuffed Bell Peppers

Servings: 4
Cooking Time: 30 minutes
Ingredients:
- 2 cups cooked quinoa
- 4 large bell peppers, halved and seeds removed
- 2 cups fresh spinach, chopped
- 1 cup crumbled feta cheese
- 1/2 cup cherry tomatoes, diced
- 1/4 cup Kalamata olives, sliced
- 2 cloves garlic, minced
- 1 teaspoon dried oregano
- 1/2 teaspoon red pepper flakes (optional)
- Salt and pepper to taste
- Olive oil for drizzling

Instructions:
1. Preheat the oven to 375°F (190°C).
2. In a large mixing bowl, combine cooked quinoa, chopped spinach, feta cheese,

cherry tomatoes, olives, garlic, oregano, red pepper flakes (if using), salt, and pepper.

3. Drizzle the bell peppers with olive oil and place them in a baking dish.
4. Stuff each pepper half with the quinoa mixture, pressing down gently.
5. Bake in the preheated oven for 20-25 minutes or until the peppers are tender.
6. Serve hot, optionally garnished with additional feta and a sprinkle of oregano.

Nutritional Values (per serving):
- Calories: 320
- Fat: 12g
- Carbs: 42g
- Protein: 12.5g

Lemon-Herb Bulgur Pilaf

Servings: 4
Cooking Time: 30 minutes
Ingredients:
- 1 cup coarse bulgur
- 2 cups vegetable broth
- Zest of 1 lemon
- 2 tablespoons fresh lemon juice
- 2 tablespoons olive oil
- 2 cloves garlic, minced
- 1 teaspoon dried oregano
- 1 teaspoon dried thyme
- Salt and pepper to taste
- 1/4 cup fresh parsley, chopped

Instructions:
1. In a saucepan, bring the vegetable broth to a boil.
2. Add bulgur to the boiling broth, cover, and reduce heat to low. Simmer for 15-20 minutes or until the bulgur is tender and liquid is absorbed.
3. In a separate pan, heat olive oil over medium heat. Add minced garlic and sauté until fragrant.
4. Fluff the cooked bulgur with a fork and transfer it to the pan with garlic.

5. Add lemon zest, lemon juice, oregano, thyme, salt, and pepper. Stir to combine and let it cook for an additional 5 minutes.
6. Remove from heat, and garnish with fresh parsley before serving.

Nutritional Values (per serving):
- Calories: 220
- Fat: 7g
- Carbs: 35g
- Protein: 6g

White Bean and Rosemary Hummus

Servings: 6
Cooking Time: 15 minutes
Ingredients:
- 1 can (15 oz) cannellini beans, drained and rinsed
- 2 tablespoons tahini
- 3 tablespoons olive oil
- 1 clove garlic, minced
- Juice of 1 lemon
- 1 teaspoon fresh rosemary, finely chopped
- Salt and pepper to taste
- Fresh rosemary sprigs for garnish

Instructions:
1. In a food processor, combine cannellini beans, tahini, olive oil, minced garlic, lemon juice, and chopped rosemary.
2. Process until smooth, scraping down the sides as needed. If the mixture is too thick, add a bit of water to reach the desired consistency.
3. Season with salt and pepper to taste. Blend again to incorporate the seasoning.
4. Transfer the hummus to a serving bowl, drizzle with a little extra olive oil, and garnish with fresh rosemary sprigs.
5. Serve with pita bread, vegetable sticks, or your favorite crackers.

Nutritional Values (per serving):
- Calories: 150
- Fat: 10g

- Carbs: 12g
- Protein: 4g

Mediterranean Stuffed Acorn Squash

Servings: 4
Cooking Time: 30 minutes
Ingredients:
- 2 acorn squash, halved and seeds removed
- 1 cup quinoa, cooked
- 1 can (15 oz) chickpeas, drained and rinsed
- 1 cup cherry tomatoes, halved
- 1/2 cup Kalamata olives, sliced
- 1/4 cup red onion, finely chopped
- 2 tablespoons feta cheese, crumbled
- 2 tablespoons fresh parsley, chopped
- 2 tablespoons olive oil
- 1 teaspoon dried oregano
- Salt and pepper to taste

Instructions:
1. Preheat the oven to 400°F (200°C).
2. Place the acorn squash halves on a baking sheet, cut side up. Drizzle with olive oil and season with salt and pepper. Roast for 20-25 minutes or until tender.
3. In a large bowl, combine cooked quinoa, chickpeas, cherry tomatoes, Kalamata olives, red onion, feta cheese, and fresh parsley.
4. Drizzle olive oil over the quinoa mixture, add dried oregano, and toss to combine. Season with salt and pepper to taste.
5. Spoon the quinoa mixture into the roasted acorn squash halves.
6. Place the stuffed squash back in the oven for an additional 5 minutes.
7. Remove from the oven, garnish with extra parsley if desired, and serve.

Nutritional Values (per serving):
- Calories: 380
- Fat: 15g
- Carbs: 55g
- Protein: 11g

Herbed Couscous with Roasted Vegetables

Servings: 4
Cooking Time: 30 minutes
Ingredients:
- 1 cup couscous
- 2 cups mixed vegetables (zucchini, bell peppers, cherry tomatoes), chopped
- 3 tablespoons olive oil
- 1 teaspoon dried thyme
- 1 teaspoon dried rosemary
- 1 teaspoon garlic powder
- Salt and pepper to taste
- Fresh parsley for garnish

Instructions:
1. Preheat the oven to 425°F (220°C).
2. Place chopped vegetables on a baking sheet. Drizzle with 2 tablespoons of olive oil, sprinkle dried thyme, rosemary, garlic powder, salt, and pepper. Toss to coat evenly.
3. Roast the vegetables in the oven for 20-25 minutes or until they are golden brown and tender.
4. While the vegetables are roasting, prepare the couscous according to package instructions.
5. In a large bowl, fluff the cooked couscous with a fork. Add the roasted vegetables and drizzle with the remaining olive oil.
6. Toss everything together until well combined. Garnish with fresh parsley.
7. Serve warm as a side dish or a light main course.

Nutritional Values (per serving):
- Calories: 280
- Fat: 10g
- Carbs: 42g
- Protein: 6g

Eggplant and Tomato Lentil Stew

Servings: 6
Cooking Time: 30 minutes
Ingredients:

- 1 cup brown lentils, rinsed
- 1 large eggplant, diced
- 1 onion, finely chopped
- 3 cloves garlic, minced
- 1 can (14 oz) diced tomatoes
- 4 cups vegetable broth
- 2 teaspoons ground cumin
- 1 teaspoon paprika
- 1/2 teaspoon cinnamon
- Salt and pepper to taste
- Fresh parsley for garnish

Instructions:

1. In a large pot, sauté the chopped onion and minced garlic over medium heat until softened.
2. Add the diced eggplant and continue to cook for 5 minutes until it starts to brown.
3. Stir in the ground cumin, paprika, and cinnamon, coating the vegetables evenly.
4. Pour in the vegetable broth, add the rinsed lentils, and bring the stew to a simmer.
5. Cover the pot and let it cook for 20-25 minutes or until lentils are tender.
6. Add the diced tomatoes with their juice and season with salt and pepper. Simmer for an additional 5 minutes.
7. Adjust the seasoning if needed and serve hot, garnished with fresh parsley.

Nutritional Values (per serving):

- Calories: 220
- Fat: 1g
- Carbs: 45g
- Protein: 10g

Olive and Sun-Dried Tomato Polenta

Servings: 4
Cooking Time: 30 minutes

Ingredients:

- 1 cup cornmeal
- 4 cups vegetable broth
- 1/2 cup grated Parmesan cheese
- 1/2 cup sliced Kalamata olives
- 1/4 cup chopped sun-dried tomatoes (packed in oil)
- 2 tablespoons olive oil
- 2 cloves garlic, minced
- Salt and pepper to taste
- Fresh basil for garnish

Instructions:

1. In a saucepan, bring the vegetable broth to a boil. Slowly whisk in the cornmeal to avoid lumps.
2. Reduce heat to low and continue stirring until the polenta thickens, about 15-20 minutes.
3. Stir in the grated Parmesan cheese, sliced olives, and chopped sun-dried tomatoes.
4. In a separate pan, sauté minced garlic in olive oil until fragrant, then add it to the polenta.
5. Season with salt and pepper to taste and stir until well combined.
6. Cook for an additional 5 minutes until the polenta reaches a creamy consistency.
7. Serve warm, garnished with fresh basil.

Nutritional Values (per serving):

- Calories: 280
- Fat: 12g
- Carbs: 35g
- Protein: 8g

Mediterranean Brown Rice Pilaf

Servings: 4
Cooking Time: 30 minutes
Ingredients:

- 1 cup brown rice
- 2 cups vegetable broth
- 1/2 cup diced tomatoes
- 1/4 cup chopped green olives
- 1/4 cup chopped roasted red peppers

- 1/4 cup chopped fresh parsley
- 2 tablespoons olive oil
- 2 cloves garlic, minced
- 1 teaspoon dried oregano
- Salt and pepper to taste
- Lemon wedges for serving

Instructions:
1. Rinse the brown rice under cold water.
2. In a saucepan, combine brown rice and vegetable broth. Bring to a boil, then reduce heat, cover, and simmer for 25-30 minutes or until rice is tender.
3. In a skillet, heat olive oil over medium heat. Add minced garlic and sauté until fragrant.
4. Add diced tomatoes, green olives, roasted red peppers, and dried oregano to the skillet. Cook for 5 minutes.
5. Fluff the cooked brown rice with a fork and add it to the skillet. Toss everything together.
6. Season with salt and pepper to taste. Garnish with chopped parsley.
7. Serve warm with lemon wedges on the side.

Nutritional Values (per serving):
- Calories: 240
- Fat: 8g
- Carbs: 38g
- Protein: 5g

Mediterranean Three-Bean Salad

Servings: 6
Cooking Time: 15 minutes
Ingredients:
- 1 can (15 oz) chickpeas, drained and rinsed
- 1 can (15 oz) kidney beans, drained and rinsed
- 1 can (15 oz) black beans, drained and rinsed
- 1/2 red onion, finely chopped
- 1 cup cherry tomatoes, halved
- 1/2 cup Kalamata olives, sliced
- 1/4 cup fresh parsley, chopped
- 1/4 cup feta cheese, crumbled

- 3 tablespoons extra-virgin olive oil
- 2 tablespoons red wine vinegar
- 1 teaspoon dried oregano
- Salt and pepper to taste

Instructions:
1. In a large bowl, combine chickpeas, kidney beans, black beans, red onion, cherry tomatoes, Kalamata olives, and parsley.
2. In a small bowl, whisk together olive oil, red wine vinegar, dried oregano, salt, and pepper.
3. Pour the dressing over the bean mixture and toss gently to combine.
4. Sprinkle crumbled feta cheese on top.
5. Allow the salad to marinate for at least 10 minutes before serving.
6. Serve chilled as a refreshing side dish or a light main course.

Nutritional Values (per serving):
- Calories: 280
- Fat: 12g
- Carbs: 32g
- Protein: 10g

Greek Chickpea and Spinach Casserole

Servings: 4
Cooking Time: 25 minutes
Ingredients:
- 2 cans (15 oz each) chickpeas, drained and rinsed
- 1 lb fresh spinach, chopped
- 1 cup cherry tomatoes, halved
- 1/2 cup feta cheese, crumbled
- 1/4 cup Kalamata olives, sliced
- 3 cloves garlic, minced
- 2 tablespoons olive oil
- 1 tablespoon lemon juice
- 1 teaspoon dried oregano
- Salt and pepper to taste

Instructions:
1. Preheat the oven to 375°F (190°C).

2. In a large oven-safe skillet, sauté minced garlic in olive oil until fragrant.
3. Add chopped spinach and cook until wilted.
4. Stir in chickpeas, cherry tomatoes, feta cheese, and Kalamata olives.
5. Drizzle lemon juice over the mixture, sprinkle with dried oregano, salt, and pepper.
6. Transfer the skillet to the preheated oven and bake for 15 minutes or until the casserole is heated through.
7. Broil for an additional 3-5 minutes until the top is lightly browned.
8. Remove from the oven, let it cool slightly, and serve.

Nutritional Values (per serving):
- Calories: 320
- Fat: 14g
- Carbs: 38g
- Protein: 14g

Spinach and Artichoke Orzo Salad

Servings: 6
Cooking Time: 20 minutes
Ingredients:
- 1 cup orzo pasta
- 1 can (14 oz) artichoke hearts, drained and chopped
- 2 cups fresh spinach, chopped
- 1/2 cup feta cheese, crumbled
- 1/4 cup red onion, finely chopped
- 1/4 cup sun-dried tomatoes, chopped
- 2 tablespoons extra-virgin olive oil
- 1 tablespoon balsamic vinegar
- 1 teaspoon Dijon mustard
- Salt and pepper to taste

Instructions:
1. Cook orzo pasta according to package instructions. Drain and let it cool.
2. In a large bowl, combine cooked orzo, chopped artichoke hearts, fresh spinach, feta cheese, red onion, and sun-dried tomatoes.
3. In a small bowl, whisk together olive oil, balsamic vinegar, Dijon mustard, salt, and pepper.
4. Pour the dressing over the orzo mixture and toss until well combined.
5. Refrigerate for at least 30 minutes before serving to allow flavors to meld.
6. Serve chilled and enjoy!

Nutritional Values (per serving):
- Calories: 280
- Fat: 12g
- Carbs: 36g
- Protein: 8g

PASTA

Mediterranean Lemon-Garlic Shrimp Pasta

Servings: 4
Cooking Time: 20 minutes
Ingredients:
- 8 oz whole wheat linguine
- 1 lb large shrimp, peeled and deveined
- 4 tbsp olive oil
- 4 cloves garlic, minced
- 1 pint cherry tomatoes, halved
- 1/2 cup Kalamata olives, pitted and sliced
- 1/4 cup fresh parsley, chopped
- 1 lemon, zest and juice
- Salt and black pepper to taste
- Crushed red pepper flakes (optional)

Instructions:
1. Cook the linguine according to package instructions. Drain and set aside.
2. In a large skillet, heat olive oil over medium heat. Add minced garlic and sauté until fragrant.
3. Add shrimp to the skillet and cook until they turn pink, about 2-3 minutes per side.
4. Stir in cherry tomatoes and Kalamata olives, cooking until the tomatoes soften.
5. Toss in the cooked linguine, ensuring it's well-coated with the shrimp and vegetable mixture.
6. Add lemon zest, lemon juice, and chopped parsley. Season with salt and black pepper to taste. For some heat, add crushed red pepper flakes if desired.
7. Mix everything together until the flavors meld.
8. Serve immediately, garnished with additional parsley and a wedge of lemon if desired.

Nutritional Values (per serving):
- Calories: 480
- Fat: 18g
- Carbs: 54g
- Protein: 28g

Greek Pasta Salad with Cherry Tomatoes and Feta

Servings: 6
Cooking Time: 15 minutes
Ingredients:
- 12 oz whole wheat fusilli pasta
- 1 cup cherry tomatoes, halved
- 1 cucumber, diced
- 1/2 red onion, thinly sliced
- 1/2 cup Kalamata olives, pitted and sliced
- 1/2 cup crumbled feta cheese
- 1/4 cup fresh parsley, chopped
- 1/4 cup extra-virgin olive oil
- 2 tbsp red wine vinegar
- 1 tsp dried oregano
- Salt and black pepper to taste

Instructions:
1. Cook the fusilli pasta according to package instructions. Drain and let it cool.
2. In a large bowl, combine the cooked pasta, cherry tomatoes, cucumber, red onion, Kalamata olives, feta cheese, and fresh parsley.
3. In a small bowl, whisk together olive oil, red wine vinegar, dried oregano, salt, and black pepper.
4. Pour the dressing over the pasta mixture and toss until everything is well-coated.
5. Adjust seasoning if needed.
6. Chill in the refrigerator for at least 30 minutes before serving to allow flavors to meld.

7. Serve as a refreshing side dish or a light main course.

Nutritional Values (per serving):
- Calories: 350
- Fat: 16g
- Carbs: 42g
- Protein: 10g

Spaghetti Aglio e Olio with Olives and Tomatoes

Servings: 4
Cooking Time: 20 minutes
Ingredients:
- 12 oz whole wheat spaghetti
- 1/4 cup extra-virgin olive oil
- 4 cloves garlic, thinly sliced
- 1/2 tsp red pepper flakes (optional)
- 1 cup cherry tomatoes, halved
- 1/2 cup Kalamata olives, pitted and sliced
- Salt and black pepper to taste
- Fresh parsley, chopped, for garnish
- Grated Parmesan cheese (optional)

Instructions:
1. Cook the spaghetti according to package instructions. Drain and set aside.
2. In a large skillet, heat olive oil over medium heat. Add sliced garlic and red pepper flakes (if using) and sauté until garlic is golden but not browned.
3. Add cherry tomatoes and Kalamata olives to the skillet. Cook for 3-5 minutes until tomatoes soften.
4. Toss in the cooked spaghetti and stir to combine. Season with salt and black pepper.
5. Garnish with fresh parsley and Parmesan cheese if desired.
6. Serve immediately as a simple and flavorful pasta dish.

Nutritional Values (per serving):
- Calories: 380
- Fat: 14g
- Carbs: 54g
- Protein: 10g

Mediterranean Chicken Pesto Pasta

Servings: 4
Cooking Time: 25 minutes
Ingredients:
- 8 oz whole wheat penne pasta
- 1 lb boneless, skinless chicken breasts, cut into bite-sized pieces
- Salt and black pepper to taste
- 2 tbsp olive oil
- 3 cloves garlic, minced
- 1 cup cherry tomatoes, halved
- 1/2 cup black olives, sliced
- 1/4 cup sun-dried tomatoes, chopped
- 1/2 cup basil pesto
- 1/4 cup grated Parmesan cheese
- Fresh basil, chopped, for garnish (optional)

Instructions:
1. Cook the penne pasta according to package instructions. Drain and set aside.
2. Season the chicken pieces with salt and black pepper.
3. In a large skillet, heat olive oil over medium-high heat. Add the seasoned chicken and cook until browned and cooked through.
4. Add minced garlic to the skillet and sauté for 1-2 minutes until fragrant.
5. Stir in cherry tomatoes, black olives, and sun-dried tomatoes. Cook for an additional 3-5 minutes.
6. Add the cooked pasta to the skillet and toss with basil pesto until everything is well coated.
7. Garnish with grated Parmesan cheese and fresh basil if desired.
8. Serve warm for a delicious Mediterranean-inspired chicken pesto pasta.

Nutritional Values (per serving):
- Calories: 520
- Fat: 25g
- Carbs: 45g
- Protein: 30g

Spinach and Feta Stuffed Shells

Servings: 4
Cooking Time: 30 minutes
Ingredients:

- 20 jumbo pasta shells
- 2 cups fresh spinach, chopped
- 1 cup feta cheese, crumbled
- 1 cup ricotta cheese
- 1 egg, beaten
- 2 cloves garlic, minced
- 1/2 teaspoon dried oregano
- Salt and black pepper to taste
- 2 cups marinara sauce
- 1/2 cup shredded mozzarella cheese
- Fresh basil, chopped, for garnish (optional)

Instructions:

1. Cook the jumbo pasta shells according to package instructions. Drain and set aside.
2. Preheat the oven to 375°F (190°C).
3. In a large mixing bowl, combine chopped spinach, feta cheese, ricotta cheese, beaten egg, minced garlic, dried oregano, salt, and black pepper. Mix well.
4. Stuff each pasta shell with the spinach and feta mixture.
5. Spread a thin layer of marinara sauce on the bottom of a baking dish.
6. Arrange the stuffed shells in the baking dish, then pour the remaining marinara sauce over the top.
7. Sprinkle shredded mozzarella cheese evenly over the shells.
8. Bake in the preheated oven for 20-25 minutes or until the cheese is melted and bubbly.
9. Garnish with fresh basil if desired.
10. Serve warm for a delightful dish of Mediterranean-inspired spinach and feta stuffed shells.

Nutritional Values (per serving):

- Calories: 450
- Fat: 18g
- Carbs: 50g
- Protein: 22g

Roasted Red Pepper and Artichoke Penne

Servings: 4
Cooking Time: 30 minutes
Ingredients:

- 8 oz penne pasta
- 1 cup roasted red peppers, sliced
- 1 cup artichoke hearts, quartered
- 3 cloves garlic, minced
- 1/4 cup Kalamata olives, sliced
- 2 tablespoons capers
- 1/4 cup extra-virgin olive oil
- 1 teaspoon dried oregano
- Salt and black pepper to taste
- 1/2 cup crumbled feta cheese
- Fresh parsley, chopped, for garnish

Instructions:

1. Cook the penne pasta according to package instructions. Drain and set aside.
2. In a large skillet over medium heat, add extra-virgin olive oil. Sauté minced garlic until fragrant.
3. Add roasted red peppers, artichoke hearts, Kalamata olives, and capers to the skillet. Cook for 5-7 minutes, stirring occasionally.
4. Season the mixture with dried oregano, salt, and black pepper. Stir well.
5. Add the cooked penne pasta to the skillet and toss to combine, ensuring the pasta is well-coated with the sauce.
6. Sprinkle crumbled feta cheese over the top and gently mix.
7. Garnish with fresh parsley.
8. Serve the Roasted Red Pepper and Artichoke Penne warm, showcasing the flavors of the Mediterranean.

Nutritional Values (per serving):

- Calories: 380
- Fat: 18g
- Carbs: 45g

- Protein: 10g

Shrimp and Olive Linguine with Tomato Sauce

Servings: 4
Cooking Time: 30 minutes
Ingredients:
- 8 oz linguine pasta
- 1 pound shrimp, peeled and deveined
- 2 tablespoons olive oil
- 3 cloves garlic, minced
- 1 can (14 oz) diced tomatoes
- 1/2 cup Kalamata olives, sliced
- 1 teaspoon dried basil
- 1/2 teaspoon red pepper flakes (optional)
- Salt and black pepper to taste
- Fresh parsley, chopped, for garnish
- Grated Parmesan cheese (optional)

Instructions:
1. Cook the linguine pasta according to package instructions. Drain and set aside.
2. In a large skillet over medium heat, add olive oil. Sauté minced garlic until fragrant.
3. Add shrimp to the skillet and cook until pink and opaque.
4. Pour in the diced tomatoes, including the juice, and add Kalamata olives, dried basil, red pepper flakes (if using), salt, and black pepper. Simmer for 10 minutes.
5. Toss the cooked linguine into the skillet, ensuring it's well-coated with the tomato and shrimp sauce.
6. Garnish with fresh parsley and, if desired, sprinkle with grated Parmesan cheese.
7. Serve the Shrimp and Olive Linguine warm, delivering a delightful Mediterranean-inspired pasta dish.

Nutritional Values (per serving):
- Calories: 420
- Fat: 12g
- Carbs: 54g
- Protein: 25g

Mediterranean Zucchini Noodle Bowl

Servings: 2
Cooking Time: 20 minutes
Ingredients:
- 2 large zucchinis, spiralized
- 1 cup cherry tomatoes, halved
- 1/2 cup cucumber, diced
- 1/4 cup red onion, finely chopped
- 1/4 cup Kalamata olives, sliced
- 2 tablespoons extra-virgin olive oil
- 1 tablespoon balsamic vinegar
- 1 teaspoon dried oregano
- Salt and black pepper to taste
- Feta cheese, crumbled, for garnish
- Fresh basil, chopped, for garnish

Instructions:
1. In a large bowl, combine the zucchini noodles, cherry tomatoes, cucumber, red onion, and Kalamata olives.
2. In a small bowl, whisk together the olive oil, balsamic vinegar, dried oregano, salt, and black pepper to create the dressing.
3. Pour the dressing over the zucchini noodle mixture and toss until well-coated.
4. Allow the flavors to meld for a few minutes before serving.
5. Garnish with crumbled feta cheese and fresh basil.
6. Serve the Mediterranean Zucchini Noodle Bowl as a refreshing and low-carb alternative, perfect for a quick and healthy meal.

Nutritional Values (per serving):
- Calories: 210
- Fat: 17g
- Carbs: 14g
- Protein: 5g

Greek Orzo Pasta with Spinach and Feta

Servings: 4

Cooking Time: 15 minutes

Ingredients:

- 8 oz orzo pasta
- 2 cups fresh spinach, chopped
- 1 cup cherry tomatoes, halved
- 1/2 cup crumbled feta cheese
- 1/4 cup Kalamata olives, sliced
- 2 tablespoons extra-virgin olive oil
- 1 tablespoon lemon juice
- 1 teaspoon dried oregano
- Salt and black pepper to taste
- Fresh parsley, chopped, for garnish

Instructions:

1. Cook the orzo pasta according to package instructions. Drain and set aside.
2. In a large bowl, combine the cooked orzo, fresh spinach, cherry tomatoes, feta cheese, and Kalamata olives.
3. In a small bowl, whisk together the olive oil, lemon juice, dried oregano, salt, and black pepper to create the dressing.
4. Pour the dressing over the orzo mixture and toss until well-combined.
5. Garnish with fresh parsley before serving.
6. Enjoy this Greek-inspired orzo pasta dish as a delightful and flavorful option for a quick meal.

Nutritional Values (per serving):

- Calories: 320
- Fat: 12g
- Carbs: 45g
- Protein: 10g

Sun-Dried Tomato and Basil Pesto Cavatappi

Servings: 4

Cooking Time: 20 minutes

Ingredients:

- 8 oz cavatappi pasta
- 1/2 cup sun-dried tomatoes, packed in oil, drained and chopped
- 1/3 cup pine nuts
- 2 cups fresh basil leaves
- 2 cloves garlic, minced
- 1/2 cup grated Parmesan cheese
- 1/2 cup extra-virgin olive oil
- Salt and black pepper to taste
- Grated Parmesan for garnish

Instructions:

1. Cook the cavatappi pasta according to package instructions. Drain and set aside.
2. In a food processor, combine sun-dried tomatoes, pine nuts, basil, garlic, and Parmesan cheese. Pulse until coarsely chopped.
3. With the processor running, slowly pour in the olive oil until the pesto reaches a smooth consistency.
4. Season the pesto with salt and black pepper to taste.
5. Toss the cooked cavatappi with the sun-dried tomato and basil pesto until well-coated.
6. Garnish with additional grated Parmesan before serving.
7. Indulge in the rich flavors of this Sun-Dried Tomato and Basil Pesto Cavatappi.

Nutritional Values (per serving):

- Calories: 540
- Fat: 38g
- Carbs: 42g
- Protein: 12g

Lemon and Herb Fettuccine with Grilled Vegetables

Servings: 4

Cooking Time: 25 minutes

Ingredients:

- 8 oz fettuccine pasta
- 1 zucchini, sliced
- 1 red bell pepper, sliced
- 1 yellow bell pepper, sliced
- 1 red onion, thinly sliced
- 2 tablespoons olive oil
- Zest and juice of 1 lemon

- 2 cloves garlic, minced
- 2 tablespoons fresh basil, chopped
- Salt and black pepper to taste
- Grated Parmesan cheese for garnish

Instructions:
1. Cook the fettuccine pasta according to package instructions. Drain and set aside.
2. In a bowl, toss zucchini, red and yellow bell peppers, and red onion with olive oil.
3. Grill the vegetables over medium-high heat until tender and slightly charred.
4. In a separate bowl, combine lemon zest, lemon juice, minced garlic, and fresh basil to create the herb dressing.
5. Toss the cooked fettuccine with grilled vegetables and herb dressing.
6. Season with salt and black pepper to taste.
7. Serve the Lemon and Herb Fettuccine with a sprinkle of grated Parmesan cheese.

Nutritional Values (per serving):
- Calories: 380
- Fat: 14g
- Carbs: 55g
- Protein: 10g

Mediterranean Sausage and Eggplant Rigatoni

Servings: 4
Cooking Time: 30 minutes
Ingredients:
- 8 oz rigatoni pasta
- 1/2 lb Italian sausage, casing removed
- 1 small eggplant, diced
- 1 can (14 oz) diced tomatoes, undrained
- 2 cloves garlic, minced
- 1 teaspoon dried oregano
- 1 teaspoon dried basil
- Salt and black pepper to taste
- 2 tablespoons olive oil
- Fresh parsley, chopped, for garnish
- Grated Parmesan cheese for serving

Instructions:
1. Cook the rigatoni pasta according to package instructions. Drain and set aside.
2. In a large skillet, heat olive oil over medium heat. Add Italian sausage and cook until browned, breaking it into crumbles.
3. Add diced eggplant to the skillet and cook until softened.
4. Stir in minced garlic, dried oregano, dried basil, salt, and black pepper.
5. Pour in diced tomatoes with their juices and let the mixture simmer for 10-15 minutes.
6. Toss the cooked rigatoni into the skillet, coating it evenly with the sauce.
7. Garnish with fresh parsley and serve with grated Parmesan cheese.

Nutritional Values (per serving):
- Calories: 480
- Fat: 18g
- Carbs: 58g
- Protein: 20g

Cherry Tomato and Kalamata Olive Linguine

Servings: 4
Cooking Time: 30 minutes
Ingredients:
- 8 oz linguine pasta
- 2 tablespoons olive oil
- 2 cloves garlic, minced
- 1 pint cherry tomatoes, halved
- 1/2 cup Kalamata olives, pitted and sliced
- 1 teaspoon dried oregano
- 1/4 teaspoon red pepper flakes (optional)
- Salt and black pepper to taste
- Fresh basil, chopped, for garnish
- Feta cheese, crumbled, for serving

Instructions:
1. Cook the linguine pasta according to package instructions. Drain and set aside.
2. In a large skillet, heat olive oil over medium heat. Add minced garlic and sauté until fragrant.

3. Add cherry tomatoes, Kalamata olives, dried oregano, red pepper flakes (if using), salt, and black pepper. Cook until tomatoes are softened.
4. Toss the cooked linguine into the skillet, ensuring it's well-coated with the tomato and olive mixture.
5. Garnish with fresh chopped basil and crumbled Feta cheese before serving.

Nutritional Values (per serving):
- Calories: 380
- Fat: 14g
- Carbs: 54g
- Protein: 10g

Feta and Spinach Stuffed Manicotti

Servings: 4
Cooking Time: 30 minutes
Ingredients:
- 8 manicotti shells
- 2 cups fresh spinach, chopped
- 1 cup Feta cheese, crumbled
- 1/2 cup ricotta cheese
- 1 egg
- 1 clove garlic, minced
- 1/4 teaspoon nutmeg
- Salt and black pepper to taste
- 2 cups marinara sauce
- 1 cup mozzarella cheese, shredded
- Fresh basil, chopped, for garnish

Instructions:
1. Preheat the oven to 375°F (190°C).
2. Cook the manicotti shells according to package instructions. Drain and set aside.
3. In a bowl, combine chopped spinach, Feta cheese, ricotta cheese, egg, minced garlic, nutmeg, salt, and black pepper. Mix well.
4. Using a piping bag or spoon, stuff each manicotti shell with the spinach and Feta mixture.

5. Spread a thin layer of marinara sauce in a baking dish. Place the stuffed manicotti in the dish.
6. Pour the remaining marinara sauce over the manicotti and sprinkle with mozzarella cheese.
7. Bake in the preheated oven for 20-25 minutes or until the cheese is melted and bubbly.
8. Garnish with fresh chopped basil before serving.

Nutritional Values (per serving):
- Calories: 420
- Fat: 18g
- Carbs: 42g
- Protein: 22g

Pappardelle with Mediterranean Roasted Vegetable Sauce

Servings: 4
Cooking Time: 30 minutes
Ingredients:
- 8 oz pappardelle pasta
- 1 eggplant, diced
- 1 zucchini, diced
- 1 red bell pepper, diced
- 1 yellow bell pepper, diced
- 1 red onion, sliced
- 3 cloves garlic, minced
- 2 tablespoons olive oil
- 1 teaspoon dried oregano
- 1 teaspoon dried basil
- Salt and black pepper to taste
- 1 can (14 oz) diced tomatoes
- 1/4 cup Kalamata olives, sliced
- 1/4 cup fresh parsley, chopped
- Grated Parmesan cheese for serving

Instructions:
1. Preheat the oven to 400°F (200°C).
2. Place diced eggplant, zucchini, red bell pepper, yellow bell pepper, and sliced red onion on a baking sheet.

3. Drizzle with olive oil, sprinkle with dried oregano, dried basil, minced garlic, salt, and black pepper. Toss to coat evenly.
4. Roast the vegetables in the preheated oven for 20-25 minutes or until they are tender and slightly caramelized.
5. While roasting, cook pappardelle pasta according to package instructions. Drain and set aside.
6. In a saucepan, combine diced tomatoes and Kalamata olives. Heat over medium heat until warmed through.
7. Mix the roasted vegetables with the tomato and olive sauce.
8. Serve the Mediterranean roasted vegetable sauce over the cooked pappardelle.
9. Garnish with fresh parsley and grated Parmesan cheese.

Nutritional Values (per serving):
- Calories: 380
- Fat: 10g
- Carbs: 62g
- Protein: 12g

FISH AND SEAFOOD

Grilled Mediterranean Salmon

Servings: 4
Cooking Time: 20 minutes
Ingredients:
- 4 salmon fillets (6 oz each)
- 2 tablespoons extra-virgin olive oil
- 2 tablespoons lemon juice
- 2 cloves garlic, minced
- 1 teaspoon dried oregano
- 1 teaspoon dried thyme
- Salt and black pepper to taste
- Lemon wedges for garnish
- Fresh parsley, chopped (optional)

Instructions:
1. Preheat the grill to medium-high heat.
2. In a small bowl, whisk together olive oil, lemon juice, minced garlic, oregano, thyme, salt, and black pepper.
3. Place the salmon fillets on a plate and brush both sides with the prepared marinade.
4. Grill the salmon for about 4-5 minutes per side, or until the fish easily flakes with a fork.
5. Garnish with fresh parsley and serve with lemon wedges on the side.

Nutritional Values (per serving):
- Calories: 350
- Fat: 20g
- Carbs: 2g
- Protein: 38g

Lemon-Herb Baked Cod

Servings: 4
Cooking Time: 25 minutes
Ingredients:
- 4 cod fillets (6 oz each)
- 2 tablespoons olive oil
- 2 tablespoons fresh lemon juice
- 2 teaspoons fresh thyme, chopped
- 1 teaspoon fresh rosemary, chopped
- 2 cloves garlic, minced
- Salt and black pepper to taste
- Lemon slices for garnish
- Fresh parsley, chopped (optional)

Instructions:
1. Preheat the oven to 400°F (200°C).
2. Place cod fillets on a baking sheet lined with parchment paper.
3. In a small bowl, mix olive oil, lemon juice, thyme, rosemary, minced garlic, salt, and black pepper.

4. Brush the cod fillets with the prepared mixture, ensuring they are evenly coated.
5. Bake for 15-18 minutes or until the cod is opaque and flakes easily with a fork.
6. Garnish with lemon slices and fresh parsley before serving.

Nutritional Values (per serving):
- Calories: 220
- Fat: 10g
- Carbs: 2g
- Protein: 30g

Garlic and Herb Shrimp Skewers

Servings: 4
Cooking Time: 20 minutes
Ingredients:
- 1 pound large shrimp, peeled and deveined
- 3 tablespoons olive oil
- 3 cloves garlic, minced
- 2 tablespoons fresh parsley, chopped
- 1 tablespoon fresh oregano, chopped
- 1 teaspoon lemon zest
- Salt and black pepper to taste
- Lemon wedges for serving

Instructions:
1. In a bowl, combine olive oil, minced garlic, chopped parsley, chopped oregano, lemon zest, salt, and black pepper.
2. Add the peeled and deveined shrimp to the marinade, ensuring they are well-coated. Let it marinate for 10 minutes.
3. Preheat the grill or grill pan over medium-high heat.
4. Thread the marinated shrimp onto skewers.
5. Grill the shrimp skewers for 2-3 minutes per side or until they are opaque and cooked through.
6. Serve the shrimp skewers with lemon wedges on the side.

Nutritional Values (per serving):
- Calories: 180
- Fat: 10g

- Carbs: 2g
- Protein: 20g

Mediterranean Stuffed Squid

Servings: 4
Cooking Time: 30 minutes
Ingredients:
- 8 small to medium-sized squid, cleaned
- 1 cup cooked quinoa
- 1/2 cup cherry tomatoes, diced
- 1/4 cup Kalamata olives, chopped
- 2 tablespoons feta cheese, crumbled
- 2 tablespoons fresh parsley, chopped
- 2 tablespoons olive oil
- 2 cloves garlic, minced
- 1 teaspoon dried oregano
- Salt and black pepper to taste
- Lemon wedges for serving

Instructions:
1. Preheat the oven to 375°F (190°C).
2. In a bowl, combine cooked quinoa, diced cherry tomatoes, chopped Kalamata olives, feta cheese, and fresh parsley.
3. In a small pan, heat olive oil over medium heat. Add minced garlic and cook until fragrant.
4. Add the garlic and olive oil to the quinoa mixture. Season with dried oregano, salt, and black pepper. Mix well.
5. Stuff each squid with the quinoa mixture and secure the openings with toothpicks.
6. Place the stuffed squid in a baking dish and bake for 20-25 minutes or until the squid is cooked through.
7. Serve the Mediterranean stuffed squid with lemon wedges.

Nutritional Values (per serving):
- Calories: 220
- Fat: 10g
- Carbs: 15g
- Protein: 18g

Baked Lemon Garlic Tilapia

Servings: 4
Cooking Time: 25 minutes
Ingredients:
- 4 tilapia fillets
- 2 tablespoons olive oil
- 3 cloves garlic, minced
- 1 teaspoon dried oregano
- 1 teaspoon paprika
- Zest of 1 lemon
- Juice of 1 lemon
- Salt and black pepper to taste
- Fresh parsley, chopped, for garnish

Instructions:
1. Preheat the oven to 400°F (200°C). Line a baking sheet with parchment paper.
2. Place tilapia fillets on the prepared baking sheet.
3. In a small bowl, mix olive oil, minced garlic, dried oregano, paprika, lemon zest, lemon juice, salt, and black pepper.
4. Brush the tilapia fillets with the lemon-garlic mixture, ensuring they are evenly coated.
5. Bake in the preheated oven for 15-18 minutes or until the tilapia is cooked through and flakes easily with a fork.
6. Garnish with fresh chopped parsley before serving.

Nutritional Values (per serving):
- Calories: 180
- Fat: 9g
- Carbs: 2g
- Protein: 24g

Greek Style Grilled Swordfish

Servings: 4
Cooking Time: 20 minutes
Ingredients:
- 4 swordfish steaks
- 1/4 cup olive oil
- 3 cloves garlic, minced
- 1 teaspoon dried oregano
- 1 teaspoon dried thyme
- Juice of 1 lemon
- Salt and black pepper to taste
- Fresh parsley, chopped, for garnish

Instructions:
1. Preheat the grill to medium-high heat.
2. In a small bowl, whisk together olive oil, minced garlic, dried oregano, dried thyme, lemon juice, salt, and black pepper.
3. Brush the swordfish steaks with the prepared marinade.
4. Grill the swordfish for about 4-5 minutes per side or until the fish is opaque and easily flakes with a fork.
5. Remove from the grill and sprinkle with fresh chopped parsley before serving.

Nutritional Values (per serving):
- Calories: 280
- Fat: 18g
- Carbs: 2g
- Protein: 28g

Spicy Harissa Prawns

Servings: 4
Cooking Time: 15 minutes
Ingredients:
- 1 pound large prawns, peeled and deveined
- 2 tablespoons harissa paste
- 2 tablespoons olive oil
- 1 teaspoon ground cumin
- 1 teaspoon smoked paprika
- 2 cloves garlic, minced
- Salt and black pepper to taste
- Fresh cilantro, chopped, for garnish
- Lemon wedges for serving

Instructions:
1. In a bowl, mix harissa paste, olive oil, ground cumin, smoked paprika, minced garlic, salt, and black pepper.
2. Toss the prawns in the harissa mixture, ensuring they are well coated.
3. Heat a skillet over medium-high heat. Add the marinated prawns and cook for 2-3

minutes per side or until they turn pink and opaque.

4. Sprinkle with fresh chopped cilantro before serving.
5. Serve with lemon wedges on the side.

Nutritional Values (per serving):

- Calories: 180
- Fat: 10g
- Carbs: 4g
- Protein: 20g

Mediterranean Tuna Salad

Servings: 2
Cooking Time: 15 minutes
Ingredients:

- 1 can (5 oz) tuna, drained
- 1 cup cherry tomatoes, halved
- 1/2 cucumber, diced
- 1/4 red onion, finely chopped
- 1/4 cup Kalamata olives, sliced
- 2 tablespoons extra-virgin olive oil
- 1 tablespoon red wine vinegar
- 1 teaspoon dried oregano
- Salt and black pepper to taste
- Feta cheese, crumbled, for garnish
- Fresh parsley, chopped, for garnish

Instructions:

1. In a large bowl, combine tuna, cherry tomatoes, cucumber, red onion, and Kalamata olives.
2. In a small bowl, whisk together olive oil, red wine vinegar, dried oregano, salt, and black pepper.
3. Pour the dressing over the tuna mixture and toss to coat evenly.
4. Garnish with crumbled feta cheese and chopped fresh parsley.
5. Serve chilled as a refreshing tuna salad.

Nutritional Values (per serving):

- Calories: 320
- Fat: 22g
- Carbs: 10g
- Protein: 24g

Herb-Crusted Baked Sea Bass

Servings: 2
Cooking Time: 20 minutes
Ingredients:

- 2 sea bass fillets (6 oz each)
- 2 tablespoons fresh parsley, chopped
- 1 tablespoon fresh dill, chopped
- 1 tablespoon fresh basil, chopped
- 2 cloves garlic, minced
- Zest of 1 lemon
- 2 tablespoons breadcrumbs
- 2 tablespoons olive oil
- Salt and black pepper to taste
- Lemon wedges, for serving

Instructions:

1. Preheat the oven to 400°F (200°C). Line a baking sheet with parchment paper.
2. In a bowl, combine chopped parsley, dill, basil, minced garlic, lemon zest, breadcrumbs, olive oil, salt, and black pepper.
3. Place sea bass fillets on the prepared baking sheet.
4. Press the herb mixture onto the top of each fillet, creating a crust.
5. Bake in the preheated oven for 15-18 minutes or until the fish is cooked through and flakes easily with a fork.
6. Serve the herb-crusted sea bass with lemon wedges on the side.

Nutritional Values (per serving):

- Calories: 320
- Fat: 18g
- Carbs: 7g
- Protein: 32g

Tomato and Olive Branzino

Servings: 2
Cooking Time: 25 minutes
Ingredients:

- 2 branzino fillets (8 oz each)
- 1 cup cherry tomatoes, halved

- 1/2 cup Kalamata olives, pitted and sliced
- 2 tablespoons fresh oregano, chopped
- 3 tablespoons extra-virgin olive oil
- 2 cloves garlic, minced
- Salt and black pepper to taste
- Lemon wedges, for serving

Instructions:
1. Preheat the oven to 375°F (190°C). Line a baking dish with parchment paper.
2. Place the branzino fillets in the baking dish.
3. In a bowl, combine cherry tomatoes, sliced olives, chopped oregano, minced garlic, and olive oil. Season with salt and black pepper.
4. Spoon the tomato and olive mixture over the branzino fillets.
5. Bake in the preheated oven for 20-25 minutes or until the fish is opaque and flakes easily.
6. Serve the tomato and olive branzino with lemon wedges on the side.

Nutritional Values (per serving):
- Calories: 390
- Fat: 24g
- Carbs: 8g
- Protein: 36g

Saffron-infused Seafood Paella

Servings: 4
Cooking Time: 30 minutes
Ingredients:
- 1 cup bomba or Arborio rice
- 8 large shrimp, peeled and deveined
- 1/2 lb mussels, cleaned and debearded
- 1/2 lb squid, cleaned and sliced into rings
- 1/2 cup green peas
- 1 red bell pepper, diced
- 1 onion, finely chopped
- 3 cloves garlic, minced
- 2 ripe tomatoes, diced
- 4 cups fish or vegetable broth
- 1/2 teaspoon saffron threads
- 1 teaspoon smoked paprika
- 1/4 cup fresh parsley, chopped

- Salt and black pepper to taste
- Lemon wedges, for serving

Instructions:
1. In a small bowl, steep saffron threads in 2 tablespoons of warm water.
2. In a paella pan, sauté onions and garlic in olive oil until softened.
3. Add diced tomatoes and bell pepper, cook until tomatoes break down.
4. Stir in rice, saffron infusion, smoked paprika, and season with salt and black pepper.
5. Pour in the broth and bring to a simmer. Arrange shrimp, mussels, squid, and peas evenly over the rice.
6. Simmer for 20-25 minutes until rice is cooked and absorbs the liquid.
7. Garnish with fresh parsley and serve with lemon wedges.

Nutritional Values (per serving):
- Calories: 480
- Fat: 8g
- Carbs: 70g
- Protein: 30g

Lemon-Oregano Grilled Scallops

Servings: 4
Cooking Time: 15 minutes
Ingredients:
- 1 lb fresh scallops
- 2 tablespoons olive oil
- Zest and juice of 1 lemon
- 2 cloves garlic, minced
- 1 teaspoon dried oregano
- Salt and black pepper to taste
- Fresh parsley, chopped, for garnish
- Lemon wedges, for serving

Instructions:
1. In a bowl, whisk together olive oil, lemon zest, lemon juice, minced garlic, dried oregano, salt, and black pepper.
2. Pat the scallops dry and toss them in the marinade, ensuring they are well-coated. Let them marinate for 10 minutes.

3. Preheat the grill or grill pan over medium-high heat.
4. Thread the scallops onto skewers or place them directly on the grill grates.
5. Grill the scallops for 2-3 minutes per side, or until they are opaque and grill marks form.
6. Remove from the grill, garnish with fresh parsley, and serve with lemon wedges.

Nutritional Values (per serving):
- Calories: 180
- Fat: 8g
- Carbs: 3g
- Protein: 23g

Mediterranean Crab Cakes

Servings: 4
Cooking Time: 25 minutes
Ingredients:
- 1 lb lump crabmeat, drained
- 1/4 cup breadcrumbs
- 1/4 cup finely chopped red bell pepper
- 1/4 cup finely chopped red onion
- 2 tablespoons chopped fresh parsley
- 1 clove garlic, minced
- 1 teaspoon Dijon mustard
- 1 large egg, beaten
- 1 tablespoon olive oil
- Lemon wedges, for serving

Instructions:
1. In a large bowl, gently combine crabmeat, breadcrumbs, red bell pepper, red onion, parsley, garlic, Dijon mustard, and beaten egg.
2. Form the mixture into equal-sized crab cakes.
3. Heat olive oil in a skillet over medium heat.
4. Cook the crab cakes for 3-4 minutes per side or until golden brown and heated through.
5. Serve the crab cakes with lemon wedges on the side.

Nutritional Values (per serving):
- Calories: 220
- Fat: 9g

- Carbs: 10g
- Protein: 23g

Pistachio-Crusted Halibut

Servings: 2
Cooking Time: 20 minutes
Ingredients:
- 2 halibut fillets (6 oz each)
- 1/2 cup unsalted pistachios, finely chopped
- 2 tablespoons breadcrumbs
- 1 tablespoon chopped fresh parsley
- 1 teaspoon lemon zest
- Salt and pepper to taste
- 1 tablespoon olive oil
- Lemon wedges, for serving

Instructions:
1. Preheat the oven to 400°F (200°C).
2. In a bowl, mix chopped pistachios, breadcrumbs, parsley, lemon zest, salt, and pepper.
3. Pat halibut fillets dry and coat them with the pistachio mixture, pressing gently to adhere.
4. Heat olive oil in an ovenproof skillet over medium-high heat.
5. Sear the halibut fillets for 2 minutes per side.
6. Transfer the skillet to the preheated oven and bake for an additional 10-12 minutes or until the fish flakes easily.
7. Serve with lemon wedges.

Nutritional Values (per serving):
- Calories: 380
- Fat: 24g
- Carbs: 10g
- Protein: 34g

Shrimp and Feta Orzo Pilaf

Servings: 4
Cooking Time: 25 minutes

Ingredients:

- 1 cup orzo pasta
- 1 pound large shrimp, peeled and deveined
- 1 tablespoon olive oil
- 1 onion, finely chopped
- 2 cloves garlic, minced
- 1 cup cherry tomatoes, halved
- 1/2 cup crumbled feta cheese
- 2 tablespoons chopped fresh parsley
- 1 teaspoon dried oregano
- Salt and pepper to taste
- Lemon wedges, for serving

Instructions:

1. Cook orzo according to package instructions; drain and set aside.
2. In a large skillet, heat olive oil over medium heat. Add chopped onion and cook until softened.
3. Add shrimp and garlic to the skillet; cook until shrimp turn pink, about 3-4 minutes.
4. Stir in cherry tomatoes and cook for an additional 2 minutes.
5. Add the cooked orzo to the skillet, along with crumbled feta, parsley, and dried oregano. Toss until well combined.
6. Season with salt and pepper to taste.
7. Serve warm, garnished with lemon wedges.

Nutritional Values (per serving):

- Calories: 380
- Fat: 10g
- Carbs: 45g
- Protein: 30g

MEAT AND POULTRY

Mediterranean Grilled Chicken Skewers

Servings: 4
Cooking Time: 20 minutes
Ingredients:
- 1.5 lbs boneless, skinless chicken breasts, cut into cubes
- 1/4 cup extra-virgin olive oil
- 3 cloves garlic, minced
- 1 teaspoon dried oregano
- 1 teaspoon dried thyme
- 1 teaspoon smoked paprika
- Salt and pepper, to taste
- Juice of 1 lemon
- Wooden skewers, soaked in water

Instructions:
1. In a bowl, mix olive oil, minced garlic, oregano, thyme, smoked paprika, salt, pepper, and lemon juice to create the marinade.
2. Add chicken cubes to the marinade, ensuring even coating. Cover and refrigerate for at least 15 minutes.
3. Preheat grill to medium-high heat.
4. Thread marinated chicken onto soaked wooden skewers.
5. Grill skewers for about 8-10 minutes, turning occasionally, until chicken is cooked through and has a slight char.
6. Serve the grilled chicken skewers with your favorite Mediterranean sides and enjoy!

Nutritional Values (per serving):
- Calories: 300
- Fat: 15g
- Carbs: 2g
- Protein: 35g

Lemon and Herb Roasted Lamb Chops

Servings: 4
Cooking Time: 25 minutes
Ingredients:
- 8 lamb chops
- 2 tablespoons olive oil
- 3 cloves garlic, minced
- 1 tablespoon fresh rosemary, chopped
- 1 tablespoon fresh thyme, chopped
- Zest of 1 lemon
- Juice of 1/2 lemon
- Salt and black pepper, to taste

Instructions:
1. Preheat the oven to 400°F (200°C).
2. In a small bowl, combine olive oil, minced garlic, chopped rosemary, chopped thyme, lemon zest, lemon juice, salt, and black pepper.
3. Place lamb chops on a baking sheet lined with parchment paper.
4. Brush the lamb chops with the prepared lemon and herb mixture, ensuring each chop is well coated.
5. Roast in the preheated oven for about 15-18 minutes for medium-rare, or longer according to your preference.
6. Remove from the oven and let the lamb chops rest for a few minutes before serving.

Nutritional Values (per serving):
- Calories: 350
- Fat: 25g
- Carbs: 2g
- Protein: 30g

Greek Chicken Souvlaki Pita Wraps

Servings: 4
Cooking Time: 20 minutes
Ingredients:
- 1 lb boneless, skinless chicken breasts, cut into cubes
- 2 tablespoons olive oil
- 3 cloves garlic, minced
- 1 teaspoon dried oregano
- 1 teaspoon dried thyme
- 1 teaspoon smoked paprika
- Salt and black pepper, to taste
- Juice of 1 lemon
- 4 whole wheat pita bread
- Tzatziki sauce, for serving
- Sliced tomatoes, cucumbers, and red onions for garnish

Instructions:
1. In a bowl, mix olive oil, minced garlic, dried oregano, dried thyme, smoked paprika, salt, black pepper, and lemon juice to create the marinade.
2. Add the chicken cubes to the marinade, ensuring they are well-coated. Allow it to marinate for at least 15 minutes.
3. Thread the marinated chicken onto skewers and grill over medium-high heat until fully cooked.
4. Warm the whole wheat pita bread on the grill or in a pan.
5. Assemble the wraps by placing grilled chicken inside each pita, topping with sliced tomatoes, cucumbers, red onions, and a generous drizzle of tzatziki sauce.

Nutritional Values (per serving):
- Calories: 380
- Fat: 12g
- Carbs: 40g
- Protein: 30g

Italian Herb-Marinated Steak

Servings: 2

Cooking Time: 15 minutes
Ingredients:
- 1 lb sirloin or ribeye steak
- 3 tablespoons olive oil
- 2 cloves garlic, minced
- 1 teaspoon dried oregano
- 1 teaspoon dried basil
- 1 teaspoon dried rosemary
- Salt and black pepper, to taste
- 1 tablespoon balsamic vinegar
- Fresh parsley, chopped (for garnish)

Instructions:
1. In a bowl, mix olive oil, minced garlic, dried oregano, dried basil, dried rosemary, salt, black pepper, and balsamic vinegar to create the marinade.
2. Coat the steak with the marinade, ensuring it is well-covered. Allow it to marinate for at least 10 minutes.
3. Preheat a grill or grill pan over medium-high heat.
4. Grill the steak to the desired doneness, approximately 4-5 minutes per side for medium-rare.
5. Let the steak rest for a few minutes before slicing it against the grain.
6. Garnish with chopped fresh parsley and serve.

Nutritional Values (per serving):
- Calories: 480
- Fat: 34g
- Carbs: 2g
- Protein: 40g

Turkey and Spinach Stuffed Bell Peppers

Servings: 4
Cooking Time: 30 minutes
Ingredients:
- 4 large bell peppers, halved and seeds removed
- 1 lb ground turkey
- 1 cup quinoa, cooked

- 1 cup spinach, chopped
- 1 can (14 oz) diced tomatoes, drained
- 1 teaspoon olive oil
- 1 onion, finely chopped
- 2 cloves garlic, minced
- 1 teaspoon dried oregano
- 1 teaspoon ground cumin
- Salt and black pepper, to taste
- 1 cup feta cheese, crumbled (optional)
- Fresh parsley, chopped (for garnish)

Instructions:

1. Preheat the oven to 375°F (190°C).
2. Place the halved bell peppers in a baking dish.
3. In a skillet, heat olive oil over medium heat. Add onions and garlic, sauté until softened.
4. Add ground turkey and cook until browned. Drain excess fat.
5. Stir in cooked quinoa, chopped spinach, diced tomatoes, dried oregano, ground cumin, salt, and black pepper. Cook for an additional 5 minutes.
6. Spoon the turkey and quinoa mixture into each bell pepper half.
7. Bake for 20-25 minutes or until the peppers are tender.
8. If desired, sprinkle crumbled feta cheese on top and bake for an additional 5 minutes.
9. Garnish with chopped fresh parsley before serving.

Nutritional Values (per serving):

- Calories: 380
- Fat: 14g
- Carbs: 32g
- Protein: 28g

Rosemary and Garlic Roast Pork Tenderloin

Servings: 4
Cooking Time: 30 minutes
Ingredients:

- 2 pork tenderloins (about 1 lb each)
- 3 tablespoons olive oil
- 4 cloves garlic, minced
- 1 tablespoon fresh rosemary, finely chopped
- 1 teaspoon dried thyme
- Salt and black pepper, to taste
- 1 tablespoon Dijon mustard
- 1 tablespoon honey
- 1 lemon, juiced
- Zest of 1 lemon
- Fresh rosemary sprigs (for garnish)

Instructions:

1. Preheat the oven to 425°F (220°C).
2. In a small bowl, mix olive oil, minced garlic, chopped rosemary, dried thyme, salt, and black pepper.
3. Rub the pork tenderloins with the garlic and rosemary mixture, ensuring they are well coated.
4. In a large oven-safe skillet, heat olive oil over medium-high heat. Sear the pork tenderloins on all sides until browned.
5. Transfer the skillet to the preheated oven and roast for about 20-25 minutes or until the internal temperature reaches 145°F (63°C).
6. In a small bowl, whisk together Dijon mustard, honey, lemon juice, and lemon zest.
7. Brush the mustard-honey mixture over the pork during the last 5 minutes of roasting.
8. Once cooked, let the pork rest for a few minutes before slicing.
9. Garnish with fresh rosemary sprigs before serving.

Nutritional Values (per serving):

- Calories: 320
- Fat: 14g
- Carbs: 5g
- Protein: 40g

Mediterranean Lamb Kebabs with Tzatziki

Servings: 4

Cooking Time: 30 minutes

Ingredients:

- 1.5 lbs lamb leg, cut into cubes
- 2 tablespoons olive oil
- 3 cloves garlic, minced
- 1 tablespoon fresh rosemary, chopped
- 1 teaspoon ground cumin
- 1 teaspoon smoked paprika
- Salt and black pepper, to taste
- Wooden skewers, soaked in water
- Tzatziki sauce (store-bought or homemade) for serving

Instructions:

1. In a bowl, combine olive oil, minced garlic, chopped rosemary, ground cumin, smoked paprika, salt, and black pepper to create the marinade.
2. Add the lamb cubes to the marinade, ensuring each piece is well coated. Allow it to marinate for at least 15 minutes.
3. Preheat the grill or grill pan over medium-high heat.
4. Thread the marinated lamb cubes onto the soaked wooden skewers.
5. Grill the lamb kebabs for about 10-12 minutes, turning occasionally, until they reach your desired doneness.
6. Serve the lamb kebabs with a side of tzatziki sauce for dipping.

Nutritional Values (per serving):

- Calories: 320
- Fat: 20g
- Carbs: 2g
- Protein: 35g

Balsamic-Glazed Chicken Thighs

Servings: 4

Cooking Time: 30 minutes

Ingredients:

- 4 bone-in, skin-on chicken thighs
- Salt and black pepper, to taste
- 2 tablespoons olive oil
- 1/4 cup balsamic vinegar

- 2 tablespoons honey
- 3 cloves garlic, minced
- 1 teaspoon dried oregano
- Fresh parsley, chopped, for garnish

Instructions:

1. Preheat the oven to 400°F (200°C).
2. Season the chicken thighs with salt and black pepper.
3. In an oven-safe skillet, heat olive oil over medium-high heat.
4. Place the chicken thighs skin-side down and sear for about 4-5 minutes until golden brown.
5. In a bowl, whisk together balsamic vinegar, honey, minced garlic, and dried oregano.
6. Pour the balsamic mixture over the chicken thighs.
7. Transfer the skillet to the preheated oven and bake for 20-25 minutes or until the chicken reaches an internal temperature of 165°F (74°C).
8. Garnish with chopped fresh parsley before serving.

Nutritional Values (per serving):

- Calories: 380
- Fat: 22g
- Carbs: 14g
- Protein: 28g

Moroccan Spiced Chicken Tagine

Servings: 4

Cooking Time: 30 minutes

Ingredients:

- 1.5 lbs boneless, skinless chicken thighs, cut into chunks
- 2 tablespoons olive oil
- 1 large onion, finely chopped
- 3 cloves garlic, minced
- 1 teaspoon ground cumin
- 1 teaspoon ground coriander
- 1 teaspoon ground cinnamon
- 1/2 teaspoon ground turmeric
- 1/2 teaspoon paprika

- Salt and black pepper, to taste
- 1 can (14 oz) diced tomatoes, undrained
- 1/2 cup low-sodium chicken broth
- 1/2 cup dried apricots, chopped
- 1/4 cup green olives, pitted and sliced
- Fresh cilantro, chopped, for garnish
- Cooked couscous, for serving

Instructions:
1. In a large skillet or tagine, heat olive oil over medium heat.
2. Add chopped onion and sauté until softened.
3. Add minced garlic, ground cumin, ground coriander, ground cinnamon, ground turmeric, paprika, salt, and black pepper. Sauté for 2 minutes.
4. Add chicken chunks and brown on all sides.
5. Pour in diced tomatoes with their juice and chicken broth. Stir well.
6. Add chopped apricots and sliced olives. Stir to combine.
7. Cover and simmer for 20 minutes or until chicken is cooked through.
8. Garnish with chopped fresh cilantro and serve over cooked couscous.

Nutritional Values (per serving):
- Calories: 380
- Fat: 18g
- Carbs: 28g
- Protein: 26g

Grilled Italian Sausage with Peppers and Onions

Servings: 4
Cooking Time: 30 minutes
Ingredients:
- 4 Italian sausages (about 1 lb)
- 2 tablespoons olive oil
- 2 bell peppers, thinly sliced (mix of red and green)
- 1 large onion, thinly sliced
- 3 cloves garlic, minced
- 1 teaspoon dried oregano

- Salt and black pepper, to taste
- 4 sub rolls or Italian hoagie rolls

Instructions:
1. Preheat the grill to medium-high heat.
2. Grill the sausages until fully cooked and browned on all sides.
3. In a large skillet, heat olive oil over medium heat.
4. Add sliced bell peppers and onions to the skillet. Sauté until softened.
5. Add minced garlic, dried oregano, salt, and black pepper. Stir well.
6. Slice the grilled sausages into bite-sized pieces and add them to the skillet. Cook for an additional 3-5 minutes.
7. Split the sub rolls and toast them on the grill for a minute.
8. Spoon the sausage and pepper mixture into the rolls.
9. Serve hot and enjoy this delicious Italian-inspired dish.

Nutritional Values (per serving):
- Calories: 520
- Fat: 32g
- Carbs: 36g
- Protein: 20g

Herbed Mediterranean Meatballs

Servings: 4
Cooking Time: 25 minutes
Ingredients:
- 1 lb ground beef
- 1/2 cup breadcrumbs
- 1/4 cup grated Parmesan cheese
- 1/4 cup fresh parsley, finely chopped
- 1 teaspoon dried oregano
- 1 teaspoon dried basil
- 2 cloves garlic, minced
- 1 large egg
- Salt and black pepper, to taste
- 2 tablespoons olive oil

Instructions:
1. Preheat the oven to 400°F (200°C).

2. In a large bowl, combine ground beef, breadcrumbs, Parmesan cheese, chopped parsley, dried oregano, dried basil, minced garlic, egg, salt, and black pepper. Mix until well combined.

3. Form the mixture into meatballs, about 1 inch in diameter.

4. Heat olive oil in an oven-safe skillet over medium-high heat.

5. Add meatballs to the skillet and brown on all sides, about 2-3 minutes.

6. Transfer the skillet to the preheated oven and bake for 15-18 minutes or until the meatballs are cooked through.

7. Serve the herbed Mediterranean meatballs with your favorite side dishes or over pasta.

Nutritional Values (per serving):
- Calories: 380
- Fat: 26g
- Carbs: 10g
- Protein: 25g

Lemon-Honey Glazed Salmon Burgers

Servings: 4
Cooking Time: 20 minutes
Ingredients:
- 1 lb fresh salmon fillet, skinless and boneless
- 1/4 cup breadcrumbs
- 1/4 cup red onion, finely chopped
- 1/4 cup fresh dill, chopped
- Zest of 1 lemon
- 1 tablespoon Dijon mustard
- 1 tablespoon honey
- Salt and black pepper, to taste
- 4 whole wheat burger buns
- Lettuce, tomato, and red onion slices for toppings

Instructions:
1. Cut the salmon into small chunks and place them in a food processor. Pulse until finely chopped.

2. In a large bowl, combine the chopped salmon, breadcrumbs, chopped red onion, fresh dill, lemon zest, Dijon mustard, honey, salt, and black pepper. Mix until well combined.

3. Divide the mixture into 4 portions and shape each into a patty.

4. Heat a grill or skillet over medium-high heat. Cook the salmon burgers for about 4-5 minutes per side or until cooked through.

5. Toast the whole wheat burger buns.

6. Assemble the burgers with lettuce, tomato, and red onion slices. Drizzle extra honey on top if desired.

7. Serve the lemon-honey glazed salmon burgers with a side salad.

Nutritional Values (per serving):
- Calories: 320
- Fat: 12g
- Carbs: 32g
- Protein: 22g

Chicken and Olive Cacciatore

Servings: 4
Cooking Time: 30 minutes
Ingredients:
- 4 boneless, skinless chicken breasts
- Salt and black pepper, to taste
- 2 tablespoons olive oil
- 1 onion, thinly sliced
- 2 bell peppers (any color), sliced
- 3 cloves garlic, minced
- 1 teaspoon dried oregano
- 1 teaspoon dried basil
- 1/2 teaspoon red pepper flakes (optional)
- 1 cup cherry tomatoes, halved
- 1/2 cup Kalamata olives, pitted
- 1/2 cup chicken broth
- 1/4 cup dry white wine (optional)
- Fresh parsley, chopped, for garnish

Instructions:
1. Season the chicken breasts with salt and black pepper.

2. In a large skillet, heat olive oil over medium-high heat. Add the chicken breasts and cook until browned on both sides. Remove from the skillet and set aside.
3. In the same skillet, add sliced onion and bell peppers. Cook until softened.
4. Add minced garlic, dried oregano, dried basil, and red pepper flakes. Cook for an additional 1-2 minutes.
5. Return the browned chicken to the skillet. Add cherry tomatoes, Kalamata olives, chicken broth, and white wine (if using).
6. Cover and simmer for about 20 minutes or until the chicken is cooked through.
7. Garnish with fresh parsley before serving.

Nutritional Values (per serving):
- Calories: 320
- Fat: 12g
- Carbs: 10g
- Protein: 38g

Mediterranean Stuffed Zucchini Boats with Ground Turkey

Servings: 4
Cooking Time: 30 minutes
Ingredients:
- 4 medium-sized zucchini
- 1 tablespoon olive oil
- 1 onion, finely chopped
- 2 cloves garlic, minced
- 1 pound ground turkey
- 1 teaspoon dried oregano
- 1 teaspoon dried basil
- Salt and black pepper, to taste
- 1 cup cherry tomatoes, diced
- 1/2 cup feta cheese, crumbled
- Fresh parsley, chopped, for garnish

Instructions:
1. Preheat the oven to 375°F (190°C).
2. Cut each zucchini in half lengthwise. Scoop out the center to create boat-shaped halves.

3. In a large skillet, heat olive oil over medium heat. Add chopped onion and garlic, sauté until softened.
4. Add ground turkey, dried oregano, dried basil, salt, and black pepper. Cook until the turkey is browned.
5. Stir in diced cherry tomatoes and cook for an additional 2-3 minutes.
6. Fill each zucchini boat with the turkey mixture.
7. Place the stuffed zucchini in a baking dish and bake for 20 minutes or until zucchini is tender.
8. Remove from the oven, sprinkle crumbled feta cheese on top, and garnish with fresh parsley.

Nutritional Values (per serving):
- Calories: 280
- Fat: 15g
- Carbs: 10g
- Protein: 28g

Za'atar Crusted Grilled Lamb Ribs

Servings: 4
Cooking Time: 30 minutes
Ingredients:
- 1 rack of lamb ribs, cut into individual ribs
- 2 tablespoons olive oil
- 2 tablespoons za'atar spice blend
- 1 teaspoon ground cumin
- 1 teaspoon paprika
- Salt and black pepper, to taste
- Lemon wedges, for serving
- Fresh mint, chopped, for garnish

Instructions:
1. Preheat the grill to medium-high heat.
2. In a bowl, mix olive oil, za'atar, ground cumin, paprika, salt, and black pepper to create a spice rub.
3. Coat each lamb rib with the spice rub, ensuring an even distribution.
4. Place the ribs on the preheated grill and cook for about 15-20 minutes, turning

occasionally, or until they reach the desired doneness.

5. Remove from the grill and let them rest for a few minutes.
6. Serve the za'atar crusted lamb ribs with lemon wedges on the side.
7. Garnish with freshly chopped mint.

Nutritional Values (per serving):
- Calories: 340
- Fat: 24g
- Carbs: 1g
- Protein: 28g

<u>VEGETARIAN</u>

Mediterranean Stuffed Bell Peppers with Quinoa and Chickpeas

Servings: 4
Cooking Time: 30 minutes
Ingredients:
- 4 large bell peppers, halved and seeds removed
- 1 cup quinoa, rinsed
- 2 cups vegetable broth
- 1 can (15 oz) chickpeas, drained and rinsed
- 1 cup cherry tomatoes, diced
- 1/2 cup Kalamata olives, chopped
- 1/2 cup crumbled feta cheese
- 1/4 cup fresh parsley, chopped
- 2 cloves garlic, minced
- 2 tablespoons olive oil
- 1 teaspoon dried oregano
- Salt and pepper to taste

Instructions:
1. Preheat the oven to 375°F (190°C).
2. In a saucepan, combine quinoa and vegetable broth. Bring to a boil, then reduce heat, cover, and simmer for 15-20 minutes until quinoa is cooked and liquid is absorbed.
3. In a large bowl, mix cooked quinoa, chickpeas, cherry tomatoes, olives, feta, parsley, garlic, olive oil, oregano, salt, and pepper.

4. Place bell pepper halves in a baking dish. Stuff each pepper with the quinoa mixture.
5. Cover the dish with foil and bake for 20 minutes. Remove the foil and bake for an additional 10 minutes or until peppers are tender.
6. Serve the stuffed peppers warm, garnished with additional fresh parsley if desired.

Nutritional Values (per serving):
- Calories: 380
- Fat: 15g
- Carbs: 50g
- Protein: 15g

Eggplant and Zucchini Moussaka

Servings: 6
Cooking Time: 30 minutes
Ingredients:
- 1 large eggplant, thinly sliced
- 2 zucchinis, thinly sliced
- 1 onion, finely chopped
- 3 cloves garlic, minced
- 1 lb (450g) ground lentils or meatless alternative
- 1 can (14 oz) diced tomatoes
- 1/2 cup tomato sauce
- 1 teaspoon dried oregano
- 1 teaspoon dried thyme
- Salt and pepper to taste
- 2 tablespoons olive oil
- 1 cup Greek yogurt

- 2 eggs
- 1/2 cup grated Parmesan cheese

Instructions:

1. Preheat the oven to 375°F (190°C).
2. In a large skillet, heat olive oil over medium heat. Add onions and garlic, sauté until softened.
3. Add lentils or meatless alternative, diced tomatoes, tomato sauce, oregano, thyme, salt, and pepper. Simmer for 15 minutes.
4. In a separate pan, grill or sauté eggplant and zucchini slices until lightly browned.
5. In a bowl, whisk together Greek yogurt and eggs until smooth.
6. In a baking dish, layer half of the lentil mixture, followed by a layer of grilled eggplant and zucchini. Repeat.
7. Pour the yogurt mixture over the top layer and sprinkle with Parmesan cheese.
8. Bake for 25-30 minutes until the top is golden and bubbly.
9. Let it cool for a few minutes before slicing and serving.

Nutritional Values (per serving):

- Calories: 320
- Fat: 14g
- Carbs: 35g
- Protein: 18g

Spanakorizo (Greek Spinach and Rice)

Servings: 4
Cooking Time: 25 minutes
Ingredients:

- 1 cup long-grain white rice
- 2 tablespoons olive oil
- 1 onion, finely chopped
- 2 cloves garlic, minced
- 1 pound fresh spinach, washed and chopped
- 1 can (14 oz) diced tomatoes
- 1 teaspoon dried dill
- Salt and pepper to taste
- 1 lemon, juiced

- Crumbled feta cheese for garnish (optional)

Instructions:

1. Cook rice according to package instructions and set aside.
2. In a large pan, heat olive oil over medium heat. Add chopped onions and garlic, sauté until softened.
3. Add chopped spinach to the pan, stirring until wilted.
4. Pour in diced tomatoes and dried dill. Season with salt and pepper. Simmer for 10 minutes.
5. Add the cooked rice to the spinach mixture. Mix well.
6. Squeeze lemon juice over the dish and stir.
7. Serve warm, optionally garnished with crumbled feta cheese.

Nutritional Values (per serving):

- Calories: 280
- Fat: 7g
- Carbs: 48g
- Protein: 8g

Roasted Red Pepper and Feta Hummus Wrap

Servings: 2
Cooking Time: 15 minutes
Ingredients:

- 1 cup canned chickpeas, drained and rinsed
- 1/4 cup roasted red peppers, chopped
- 2 tablespoons crumbled feta cheese
- 2 tablespoons tahini
- 1 clove garlic, minced
- 2 tablespoons lemon juice
- Salt and pepper to taste
- 2 whole wheat wraps
- 1 cup mixed salad greens
- 1/2 cucumber, thinly sliced

Instructions:

1. In a food processor, combine chickpeas, roasted red peppers, feta, tahini, garlic, lemon juice, salt, and pepper. Blend until smooth.

2. Lay out the wraps and spread the hummus mixture evenly over each.
3. Place a handful of mixed greens and a few cucumber slices in the center of each wrap.
4. Fold in the sides of the wraps and then roll tightly.
5. Slice in half and serve.

Nutritional Values (per serving):
- Calories: 380
- Fat: 18g
- Carbs: 47g
- Protein: 12g

Mediterranean Lentil and Vegetable Soup

Servings: 4
Cooking Time: 30 minutes
Ingredients:
- 1 cup dried green lentils, rinsed
- 1 onion, diced
- 2 carrots, diced
- 2 celery stalks, diced
- 3 cloves garlic, minced
- 1 can (14 oz) diced tomatoes
- 4 cups vegetable broth
- 1 teaspoon dried oregano
- 1 teaspoon ground cumin
- 1/2 teaspoon smoked paprika
- Salt and pepper to taste
- 2 cups baby spinach
- 2 tablespoons fresh lemon juice
- Fresh parsley for garnish

Instructions:
1. In a large pot, combine lentils, onion, carrots, celery, garlic, diced tomatoes, vegetable broth, oregano, cumin, smoked paprika, salt, and pepper.
2. Bring to a boil, then reduce heat and simmer for 25-30 minutes or until lentils are tender.
3. Stir in the baby spinach and cook until wilted.
4. Add fresh lemon juice and adjust seasoning if needed.

5. Serve hot, garnished with fresh parsley.

Nutritional Values (per serving):
- Calories: 240
- Fat: 1g
- Carbs: 46g
- Protein: 14g

Artichoke and Sun-Dried Tomato Stuffed Portobello Mushrooms

Servings: 2
Cooking Time: 30 minutes
Ingredients:
- 2 large portobello mushrooms
- 1/2 cup artichoke hearts, chopped
- 1/4 cup sun-dried tomatoes, chopped
- 2 cloves garlic, minced
- 1/4 cup feta cheese, crumbled
- 2 tablespoons fresh basil, chopped
- 2 tablespoons pine nuts
- Salt and pepper to taste
- 2 tablespoons olive oil

Instructions:
1. Preheat the oven to 375°F (190°C).
2. Clean the portobello mushrooms and remove the stems.
3. In a bowl, mix artichoke hearts, sun-dried tomatoes, garlic, feta cheese, basil, pine nuts, salt, and pepper.
4. Brush the portobello caps with olive oil on both sides.
5. Stuff each mushroom with the artichoke mixture.
6. Place the stuffed mushrooms on a baking sheet and bake for 20 minutes or until mushrooms are tender.
7. Serve hot, optionally garnished with extra fresh basil.

Nutritional Values (per serving):
- Calories: 280
- Fat: 22g
- Carbs: 14g
- Protein: 8g

Lemon Herb Roasted Vegetable Quinoa Bowl

Servings: 2
Cooking Time: 30 minutes
Ingredients:

- 1 cup quinoa, rinsed
- 2 cups mixed vegetables (bell peppers, cherry tomatoes, zucchini, and red onion), chopped
- 2 tablespoons olive oil
- 1 tablespoon fresh lemon juice
- 1 teaspoon dried oregano
- 1 teaspoon dried thyme
- Salt and pepper to taste
- 1/4 cup feta cheese, crumbled
- Fresh parsley for garnish

Instructions:

1. Preheat the oven to 400°F (200°C).
2. In a bowl, toss the mixed vegetables with olive oil, lemon juice, dried oregano, dried thyme, salt, and pepper.
3. Spread the vegetables on a baking sheet and roast for 20-25 minutes or until they are tender and slightly caramelized.
4. While the vegetables are roasting, cook quinoa according to package instructions.
5. Assemble the bowls by placing a serving of quinoa in each bowl, topping with roasted vegetables, and sprinkling with feta cheese.
6. Garnish with fresh parsley and serve.

Nutritional Values (per serving):

- Calories: 380
- Fat: 15g
- Carbs: 48g
- Protein: 14g

Spinach and Feta Phyllo Triangles

Servings: 4
Cooking Time: 30 minutes
Ingredients:

- 8 sheets phyllo dough, thawed
- 2 cups fresh spinach, chopped
- 1 cup feta cheese, crumbled
- 1/2 cup ricotta cheese
- 1/4 cup green onions, finely chopped
- 1 clove garlic, minced
- 2 tablespoons olive oil
- Salt and pepper to taste
- Cooking spray

Instructions:

1. Preheat the oven to 375°F (190°C).
2. In a skillet, heat olive oil over medium heat. Add garlic and sauté until fragrant.
3. Add chopped spinach to the skillet and cook until wilted. Remove from heat and let it cool.
4. In a bowl, combine the cooked spinach, feta cheese, ricotta cheese, green onions, salt, and pepper.
5. Lay out one sheet of phyllo dough, brush it lightly with olive oil, and place another sheet on top. Repeat to make a stack of 4 sheets.
6. Cut the phyllo stack into four strips. Place a spoonful of the spinach and feta mixture at the end of each strip.
7. Fold the phyllo over the filling to create a triangle shape. Continue folding until you reach the end of the strip.
8. Repeat with the remaining phyllo and filling.
9. Place the triangles on a baking sheet coated with cooking spray.
10. Bake for 15-20 minutes or until golden brown and crisp.

Nutritional Values (per serving):

- Calories: 280
- Fat: 16g
- Carbs: 26g
- Protein: 9g

Caponata: Sicilian Eggplant Salad

Servings: 6
Cooking Time: 30 minutes
Ingredients:

- 1 large eggplant, diced

- 1 can (14 oz) diced tomatoes, drained
- 1/2 cup green olives, sliced
- 1/4 cup capers, drained
- 1/4 cup red wine vinegar
- 2 tablespoons olive oil
- 1 tablespoon sugar
- 1 teaspoon dried oregano
- 1/2 teaspoon red pepper flakes
- Salt and pepper to taste
- Fresh basil for garnish

Instructions:
1. In a large skillet, heat olive oil over medium heat. Add diced eggplant and cook until softened and golden brown.
2. Add diced tomatoes, green olives, and capers to the skillet. Cook for an additional 5 minutes.
3. In a small bowl, whisk together red wine vinegar, sugar, dried oregano, red pepper flakes, salt, and pepper.
4. Pour the vinegar mixture over the eggplant mixture in the skillet. Stir to combine and let it simmer for 10-15 minutes.
5. Remove from heat and let the caponata cool to room temperature.
6. Garnish with fresh basil before serving.
7. Caponata can be served as a salad, a topping for crostini, or a side dish.

Nutritional Values (per serving):
- Calories: 120
- Fat: 7g
- Carbs: 14g
- Protein: 2g

Mediterranean Chickpea and Eggplant Casserole

Servings: 4
Cooking Time: 30 minutes
Ingredients:
- 1 large eggplant, cubed
- 1 can (15 oz) chickpeas, drained and rinsed
- 1 cup cherry tomatoes, halved
- 1/2 cup crumbled feta cheese

- 1/4 cup Kalamata olives, sliced
- 2 tablespoons olive oil
- 2 cloves garlic, minced
- 1 teaspoon dried oregano
- 1/2 teaspoon smoked paprika
- Salt and pepper to taste
- Fresh parsley for garnish

Instructions:
1. Preheat the oven to 400°F (200°C).
2. In a large bowl, toss eggplant cubes with olive oil, garlic, dried oregano, smoked paprika, salt, and pepper.
3. Spread the seasoned eggplant on a baking sheet and roast for 15-20 minutes or until golden and tender.
4. In a baking dish, combine roasted eggplant, chickpeas, cherry tomatoes, feta cheese, and Kalamata olives.
5. Bake in the preheated oven for an additional 10 minutes until the flavors meld.
6. Remove from the oven, garnish with fresh parsley, and serve.

Nutritional Values (per serving):
- Calories: 280
- Fat: 15g
- Carbs: 28g
- Protein: 10g

Greek Spanakopita Quesadillas

Servings: 2
Cooking Time: 20 minutes
Ingredients:
- 4 large whole wheat or corn tortillas
- 2 cups fresh spinach, chopped
- 1 cup feta cheese, crumbled
- 1/2 cup red onion, finely chopped
- 1/4 cup fresh dill, chopped
- 1 tablespoon olive oil
- 1 teaspoon lemon zest
- Salt and pepper to taste
- Tzatziki sauce for dipping (optional)

Instructions:

1. In a skillet over medium heat, sauté chopped spinach in olive oil until wilted. Season with salt and pepper.
2. In a mixing bowl, combine wilted spinach, feta cheese, red onion, fresh dill, and lemon zest. Mix well.
3. Lay out two tortillas and divide the spinach-feta mixture evenly over each.
4. Top with the remaining two tortillas to create quesadillas.
5. In the same skillet over medium heat, cook each quesadilla for 2-3 minutes on each side or until golden brown and the cheese is melted.
6. Slice into wedges and serve with tzatziki sauce if desired.

Nutritional Values (per serving):
- Calories: 380
- Fat: 22g
- Carbs: 32g
- Protein: 15g

Roasted Vegetable and Feta Orzo Salad

Servings: 4
Cooking Time: 25 minutes
Ingredients:
- 1 cup orzo pasta
- 1 zucchini, diced
- 1 red bell pepper, diced
- 1 yellow bell pepper, diced
- 1 red onion, finely chopped
- 1 cup cherry tomatoes, halved
- 1/2 cup crumbled feta cheese
- 2 tablespoons olive oil
- 1 teaspoon dried oregano
- Salt and pepper to taste
- Fresh basil for garnish

Instructions:
1. Preheat the oven to 400°F (200°C).
2. In a large baking pan, toss the diced zucchini, red and yellow bell peppers, and red onion with olive oil, dried oregano, salt, and pepper.
3. Roast the vegetables in the preheated oven for about 20 minutes or until they are tender and slightly caramelized.
4. Cook orzo pasta according to package instructions. Drain and let it cool.
5. In a large bowl, combine the cooked orzo, roasted vegetables, cherry tomatoes, and crumbled feta cheese. Toss gently.
6. Garnish with fresh basil before serving.

Nutritional Values (per serving):
- Calories: 320
- Fat: 12g
- Carbs: 45g
- Protein: 8g

Tomato and Olive Polenta Stacks

Servings: 4
Cooking Time: 30 minutes
Ingredients:
- 1 cup instant polenta
- 4 cups water
- 1 cup cherry tomatoes, sliced
- 1/2 cup Kalamata olives, sliced
- 1/4 cup crumbled feta cheese
- 2 tablespoons olive oil
- 1 teaspoon dried thyme
- Salt and pepper to taste
- Fresh parsley for garnish

Instructions:
1. In a medium saucepan, bring 4 cups of water to a boil. Slowly pour in the instant polenta, stirring constantly to avoid lumps. Cook according to package instructions.
2. Once the polenta is cooked, spread it evenly on a baking sheet to cool and set.
3. Using a round cookie cutter, cut the polenta into circles.
4. In a skillet, heat olive oil over medium heat. Sauté cherry tomatoes and Kalamata olives until tomatoes are slightly softened.

5. Assemble the stacks by placing a polenta round, topping it with the tomato and olive mixture, and then adding another polenta round.
6. Sprinkle crumbled feta, dried thyme, salt, and pepper over the stacks.
7. Garnish with fresh parsley before serving.

Nutritional Values (per serving):
- Calories: 280
- Fat: 10g
- Carbs: 40g
- Protein: 5g

Mediterranean Pita Bread Salad

Servings: 4
Cooking Time: 20 minutes
Ingredients:
- 2 whole wheat pita bread, cut into bite-sized pieces
- 1 cup cherry tomatoes, halved
- 1 cucumber, diced
- 1/2 red onion, finely sliced
- 1/4 cup Kalamata olives, sliced
- 1/4 cup crumbled feta cheese
- 2 tablespoons extra-virgin olive oil
- 1 tablespoon red wine vinegar
- 1 teaspoon dried oregano
- Salt and pepper to taste
- Fresh parsley for garnish

Instructions:
1. Preheat the oven to 375°F (190°C).
2. Place the pita bread pieces on a baking sheet and toast in the oven until crisp, about 10 minutes.
3. In a large bowl, combine the toasted pita bread, cherry tomatoes, cucumber, red onion, Kalamata olives, and crumbled feta.
4. In a small bowl, whisk together olive oil, red wine vinegar, dried oregano, salt, and pepper.
5. Pour the dressing over the salad and toss gently to combine.

6. Let the salad sit for a few minutes to allow the flavors to meld.
7. Garnish with fresh parsley before serving.

Nutritional Values (per serving):
- Calories: 280
- Fat: 14g
- Carbs: 32g
- Protein: 7g

Spinach and Mushroom Greek-Style Risotto

Servings: 4
Cooking Time: 25 minutes
Ingredients:
- 1 cup Arborio rice
- 4 cups vegetable broth, kept warm
- 1/2 cup dry white wine
- 1 cup baby spinach, chopped
- 1 cup cremini mushrooms, sliced
- 1/2 cup crumbled feta cheese
- 1/4 cup grated Parmesan cheese
- 1/2 onion, finely chopped
- 2 cloves garlic, minced
- 2 tablespoons extra-virgin olive oil
- 1 tablespoon fresh lemon juice
- Salt and black pepper to taste
- Fresh parsley for garnish

Instructions:
1. In a large skillet, heat olive oil over medium heat. Add chopped onions and garlic, sauté until softened.
2. Add Arborio rice to the skillet and toast for 2-3 minutes, stirring constantly.
3. Pour in the white wine and cook until it's mostly absorbed by the rice.
4. Begin adding the warm vegetable broth, one ladle at a time, stirring frequently. Allow the liquid to be absorbed before adding more.
5. When the rice is almost tender, stir in the chopped spinach and sliced mushrooms.
6. Continue adding broth until the rice is creamy and cooked to al dente.

7. Remove the skillet from heat, stir in feta and Parmesan cheese, and drizzle with fresh lemon juice.
8. Season with salt and black pepper to taste. Garnish with fresh parsley before serving.

Nutritional Values (per serving):

- Calories: 320
- Fat: 14g
- Carbs: 40g
- Protein: 9g

DESSERT

Quick Greek Yogurt Parfait

Servings: 2
Cooking Time: 10 minutes
Ingredients:
- 1 cup Greek yogurt
- 1 cup mixed berries (strawberries, blueberries, raspberries)
- 1/2 cup granola
- 2 tablespoons honey
- 1/4 cup chopped nuts (almonds, walnuts)

Instructions:
1. In two serving glasses, layer the bottom with a spoonful of Greek yogurt.
2. Add a layer of mixed berries on top of the yogurt.
3. Sprinkle a layer of granola over the berries.
4. Drizzle honey evenly over the granola layer.
5. Repeat the layers until the glasses are filled, finishing with a dollop of Greek yogurt on top.
6. Garnish with chopped nuts for added crunch.
7. Serve immediately and enjoy your quick and delicious Greek Yogurt Parfait!

Nutritional Values (per serving):
- Calories: 300
- Fat: 12g
- Carbs: 40g
- Protein: 15g

Honey and Pistachio Phyllo Cups

Servings: 12
Cooking Time: 20 minutes

Ingredients:
- 1 package (12 sheets) phyllo dough, thawed
- 1/2 cup unsalted pistachios, chopped
- 1/4 cup honey
- 2 tablespoons unsalted butter, melted
- Powdered sugar for dusting (optional)

Instructions:
1. Preheat the oven to 350°F (175°C).
2. Lay one sheet of phyllo dough on a clean surface and brush it lightly with melted butter.
3. Place another sheet on top and repeat the process until you have four layers.
4. Cut the layered phyllo into squares and press each square into a muffin tin to form cups.
5. Bake the phyllo cups in the preheated oven for about 10-12 minutes or until golden brown.
6. In a bowl, mix chopped pistachios with honey.
7. Once the phyllo cups have cooled slightly, fill each cup with the honey and pistachio mixture.
8. Optionally, dust with powdered sugar before serving.
9. Enjoy these delightful Honey and Pistachio Phyllo Cups!

Nutritional Values (per serving):
- Calories: 120
- Fat: 7g
- Carbs: 14g
- Protein: 2g

Lemon Ricotta Pancakes with Berry Compote

Servings: 4
Cooking Time: 25 minutes

Ingredients:

- 1 cup all-purpose flour
- 2 tablespoons sugar
- 1 teaspoon baking powder
- 1/2 teaspoon baking soda
- 1/4 teaspoon salt
- 3/4 cup ricotta cheese
- 1 large egg
- 1 cup milk
- Zest of 1 lemon
- 1 teaspoon vanilla extract

Berry Compote:

- 1 cup mixed berries (strawberries, blueberries, raspberries)
- 2 tablespoons honey
- 1 tablespoon fresh lemon juice

Instructions:

1. In a large bowl, whisk together flour, sugar, baking powder, baking soda, and salt.
2. In another bowl, whisk together ricotta cheese, egg, milk, lemon zest, and vanilla extract until smooth.
3. Combine the wet and dry ingredients, mixing until just combined.
4. Heat a griddle or non-stick pan over medium heat.
5. Pour 1/4 cup of batter for each pancake onto the griddle.
6. Cook until bubbles form on the surface, then flip and cook until golden brown.
7. For the compote, combine berries, honey, and lemon juice in a saucepan. Simmer for 5 minutes until the berries release their juices.
8. Serve pancakes topped with the warm berry compote.
9. Enjoy these delightful Lemon Ricotta Pancakes with Berry Compote!

Nutritional Values (per serving):

- Calories: 320
- Fat: 9g
- Carbs: 50g
- Protein: 11g

Fig and Walnut Energy Bites

Servings:12-15
Prep Time: 15 minutes
Ingredients:

- 1 cup dried figs, stems removed
- 1 cup walnuts
- 1/4 cup rolled oats
- 1 tablespoon chia seeds
- 1 tablespoon honey
- 1 teaspoon vanilla extract
- A pinch of sea salt
- Desiccated coconut (for coating)

Instructions:

1. In a food processor, combine dried figs, walnuts, rolled oats, chia seeds, honey, vanilla extract, and a pinch of sea salt.
2. Pulse until the mixture comes together and forms a sticky dough.
3. Scoop out small portions of the mixture and roll them into bite-sized balls.
4. Roll the energy bites in desiccated coconut to coat.
5. Place the energy bites on a parchment-lined tray and refrigerate for at least 30 minutes.
6. Once chilled, transfer to an airtight container for storage.
7. These Fig and Walnut Energy Bites are a nutritious and quick snack option.

Nutritional Values (per serving):

- Calories: 90
- Fat: 6g
- Carbs: 9g
- Protein: 2g

No-Bake Greek Yogurt Cheesecake

Servings:8
Prep Time: 30 minutes (plus chilling time)
Ingredients:
For the Crust:

- 1 1/2 cups graham cracker crumbs
- 1/3 cup melted unsalted butter
- 2 tablespoons honey

For the Filling:
- 2 cups Greek yogurt
- 1 cup cream cheese, softened
- 1/2 cup honey
- 1 teaspoon vanilla extract
- Zest of one lemon

Instructions:
1. In a bowl, combine graham cracker crumbs, melted butter, and honey for the crust. Press the mixture into the base of a springform pan to form an even layer. Place it in the refrigerator to set.
2. In a large mixing bowl, whisk together Greek yogurt, cream cheese, honey, vanilla extract, and lemon zest until smooth and well combined.
3. Pour the filling over the chilled crust, spreading it evenly.
4. Refrigerate the cheesecake for at least 4 hours or until set.
5. Once set, remove from the springform pan, slice, and serve chilled.
6. This No-Bake Greek Yogurt Cheesecake is a delightful and quick dessert option.

Nutritional Values (per serving):
- Calories: 350
- Fat: 23g
- Carbs: 31g
- Protein: 7g

Orange and Almond Semolina Cake

Servings:10
Prep Time: 30 minutes
Ingredients:
For the Cake:
- 1 cup fine semolina
- 1 cup almond flour
- 1 cup sugar
- 1 cup plain Greek yogurt
- 1/2 cup olive oil
- 3 large eggs
- Zest of 2 oranges

- 1 teaspoon baking powder
- 1/2 teaspoon baking soda
- 1/4 teaspoon salt

For the Syrup:
- Juice of 2 oranges
- 1/2 cup honey
- 1/4 cup water
- 1 teaspoon orange blossom water (optional)

Instructions:
1. Preheat the oven to 350°F (175°C). Grease and flour a round cake pan.
2. In a large bowl, whisk together semolina, almond flour, sugar, baking powder, baking soda, and salt.
3. In another bowl, whisk together Greek yogurt, olive oil, eggs, and orange zest.
4. Combine the wet and dry ingredients until just incorporated. Pour the batter into the prepared cake pan.
5. Bake for 25-30 minutes or until a toothpick inserted into the center comes out clean.
6. While the cake is baking, prepare the syrup. In a saucepan, combine orange juice, honey, water, and orange blossom water. Simmer for 5 minutes, then remove from heat.
7. Once the cake is done, allow it to cool for 10 minutes, then pour the syrup evenly over the warm cake.
8. Let the cake absorb the syrup before slicing. Serve and enjoy this delightful Orange and Almond Semolina Cake!

Nutritional Values (per serving):
- Calories: 280
- Fat: 14g
- Carbs: 35g
- Protein: 6g

Chocolate-Dipped Mediterranean Fruits

Servings:8
Prep Time: 30 minutes
Ingredients:

- 1 cup mixed Mediterranean fruits (strawberries, figs, apricots)
- 4 ounces dark chocolate, chopped
- 2 tablespoons chopped pistachios
- 2 tablespoons shredded coconut (unsweetened)

Instructions:

1. Wash and thoroughly dry the fruits. If using figs, cut them in halves.
2. In a heatproof bowl, melt the dark chocolate using a microwave or a double boiler.
3. Dip each fruit piece into the melted chocolate, coating about half of the fruit.
4. Place the chocolate-dipped fruits on a parchment-lined tray.
5. Sprinkle chopped pistachios and shredded coconut over the chocolate-coated portion of the fruits.
6. Allow the chocolate to set by placing the tray in the refrigerator for about 15-20 minutes.
7. Once set, transfer the chocolate-dipped fruits to a serving plate.
8. Serve and savor these delectable Chocolate-Dipped Mediterranean Fruits as a delightful dessert or sweet snack.

Nutritional Values (per serving):

- Calories: 120
- Fat: 7g
- Carbs: 15g
- Protein: 2g

Mint Chocolate Greek Yogurt Popsicles

Servings:6
Prep Time: 30 minutes (plus freezing time)
Ingredients:

- 2 cups Greek yogurt
- 1/4 cup honey
- 1 teaspoon vanilla extract
- 2 tablespoons fresh mint leaves, finely chopped
- 1/2 cup dark chocolate, melted

Instructions:

1. In a bowl, mix Greek yogurt, honey, and vanilla extract until well combined.
2. Add finely chopped mint leaves to the yogurt mixture and stir.
3. Pour the yogurt mixture into popsicle molds, leaving a little space at the top.
4. Insert popsicle sticks into the molds and freeze for at least 4 hours or until completely frozen.
5. Once the popsicles are frozen, remove them from the molds.
6. Melt dark chocolate in a heatproof bowl.
7. Dip each popsicle into the melted chocolate, covering one end.
8. Place the dipped popsicles on a tray lined with parchment paper.
9. Allow the chocolate to set by placing the tray in the freezer for an additional 15 minutes.
10. Serve these refreshing Mint Chocolate Greek Yogurt Popsicles on a hot day for a delightful treat.

Nutritional Values (per serving):

- Calories: 150
- Fat: 7g
- Carbs: 15g
- Protein: 8g

Quick Baklava Rolls

Servings:12
Prep Time: 30 minutes
Ingredients:

- 1/2 cup chopped walnuts
- 1/4 cup chopped pistachios
- 1/4 cup honey
- 1 teaspoon ground cinnamon
- 1 package phyllo dough (12 sheets)
- 1/2 cup unsalted butter, melted

Instructions:

1. Preheat the oven to 350°F (175°C). Line a baking sheet with parchment paper.

2. In a bowl, combine chopped walnuts, chopped pistachios, honey, and ground cinnamon. Mix well.
3. Lay out one sheet of phyllo dough and brush it lightly with melted butter.
4. Place another sheet of phyllo dough on top and brush with butter. Repeat this process to create a stack of 4 sheets.
5. Spread a portion of the nut mixture along one edge of the phyllo stack.
6. Roll the phyllo stack into a log, enclosing the nut mixture.
7. Cut the rolled phyllo into 3 equal-sized rolls and place them on the prepared baking sheet.
8. Repeat the process with the remaining phyllo sheets and nut mixture.
9. Bake in the preheated oven for about 15-20 minutes or until the rolls are golden brown.
10. Allow the Baklava Rolls to cool slightly before serving.

Nutritional Values (per serving):
- Calories: 180
- Fat: 12g
- Carbs: 16g
- Protein: 3g

Espresso Chocolate Mousse

Servings:4
Prep Time: 30 minutes
Ingredients:
- 1 cup semi-sweet chocolate chips
- 2 tablespoons instant espresso powder
- 2 tablespoons hot water
- 2 cups heavy whipping cream
- 1/4 cup powdered sugar
- 1 teaspoon vanilla extract
- Chocolate shavings (for garnish)

Instructions:
1. Melt the chocolate chips using a double boiler or microwave, stirring until smooth. Allow it to cool slightly.

2. Dissolve instant espresso powder in hot water, creating a concentrated espresso mixture.
3. In a bowl, whip the heavy whipping cream until soft peaks form. Gradually add powdered sugar and vanilla extract, continuing to whip until stiff peaks form.
4. Gently fold the melted chocolate into the whipped cream until well combined.
5. Add the espresso mixture to the chocolate and cream mixture, folding until smooth and uniform.
6. Divide the mousse into serving glasses or bowls.
7. Refrigerate for at least 2 hours to allow the mousse to set.
8. Garnish with chocolate shavings before serving.

Nutritional Values (per serving):
- Calories: 450
- Fat: 38g
- Carbs: 25g
- Protein: 3g

Almond Flour Olive Oil Cookies

Servings:12 cookies
Prep Time: 20 minutes
Cook Time: 10 minutes
Ingredients:
- 1 cup almond flour
- 1/4 cup extra-virgin olive oil
- 1/4 cup honey
- 1 large egg
- 1/2 teaspoon vanilla extract
- 1/4 teaspoon baking soda
- Pinch of salt
- 1/3 cup chopped almonds (optional, for texture)

Instructions:
1. Preheat the oven to 350°F (175°C) and line a baking sheet with parchment paper.

2. In a bowl, whisk together almond flour, olive oil, honey, egg, vanilla extract, baking soda, and a pinch of salt until well combined.

3. If desired, fold in chopped almonds for added texture.

4. Drop spoonfuls of cookie dough onto the prepared baking sheet, spacing them about 2 inches apart.

5. Flatten each cookie slightly with the back of a spoon.

6. Bake in the preheated oven for 8-10 minutes or until the edges are golden brown.

7. Allow the cookies to cool on the baking sheet for a few minutes before transferring them to a wire rack to cool completely.

Nutritional Values (per cookie):
- Calories: 120
- Fat: 9g
- Carbs: 8g
- Protein: 3g

Quick Berry and Mint Sorbet

Servings: 4
Prep Time: 15 minutes + Freezing time
Ingredients:
- 3 cups mixed berries (such as strawberries, blueberries, and raspberries), frozen
- 1/4 cup fresh mint leaves, packed
- 1/4 cup honey or maple syrup
- 1 tablespoon freshly squeezed lemon juice
- 1/2 cup cold water

Instructions:
1. In a blender, combine frozen berries, fresh mint leaves, honey (or maple syrup), lemon juice, and cold water.

2. Blend on high until the mixture is smooth and well combined.

3. Taste and adjust sweetness if needed by adding more honey or maple syrup.

4. Pour the sorbet mixture into a shallow dish and spread it evenly.

5. Place the dish in the freezer until the sorbet is firm.

6. Before serving, let the sorbet sit at room temperature for a few minutes to soften slightly.

7. Scoop the sorbet into bowls or cones, garnish with additional mint leaves, and enjoy!

Nutritional Values (per serving):
- Calories: 90
- Fat: 0.5g
- Carbs: 23g
- Protein: 1g

Citrus and Honey Fruit Salad

Servings: 6
Prep Time: 20 minutes
Ingredients:
- 2 oranges, peeled and segmented
- 2 grapefruits, peeled and segmented
- 1 cup strawberries, hulled and halved
- 1 cup pineapple chunks
- 1 tablespoon honey
- Fresh mint leaves for garnish

Instructions:
1. In a large bowl, combine the orange segments, grapefruit segments, strawberries, and pineapple chunks.

2. Drizzle the honey over the fruit.

3. Gently toss the fruit salad until all the fruits are coated in honey.

4. Refrigerate for at least 10 minutes to let the flavors meld.

5. Before serving, garnish with fresh mint leaves.

6. Serve chilled and enjoy this refreshing citrus and honey-infused fruit salad!

Nutritional Values (per serving):
- Calories: 80
- Fat: 0.3g
- Carbs: 20g
- Protein: 1g

Greek Yogurt with Honey and Nuts

Servings: 2
Prep Time: 5 minutes
Ingredients:
- 1 cup Greek yogurt
- 2 tablespoons honey
- 2 tablespoons mixed nuts (walnuts, almonds, or pistachios), chopped

Instructions:
1. In serving bowls, spoon out the Greek yogurt evenly.
2. Drizzle honey over each portion of yogurt.
3. Sprinkle the chopped mixed nuts on top.
4. Serve immediately and enjoy this quick and delightful Greek yogurt with honey and nut combination!

Nutritional Values (per serving):
- Calories: 220
- Fat: 10g
- Carbs: 18g
- Protein: 15g

Easy Lemon Sorbet

Servings: 4
Prep Time: 10 minutes + Freezing time
Ingredients:
- 1 cup fresh lemon juice (about 6-8 lemons)
- 1 cup water
- 1 cup granulated sugar
- Zest of 1 lemon

Instructions:
1. In a small saucepan, combine water and sugar. Heat over medium heat, stirring until the sugar dissolves. Allow the syrup to cool.
2. Mix the fresh lemon juice and lemon zest into the cooled sugar syrup.
3. Pour the mixture into a shallow, freezer-safe dish.
4. Freeze for about 1 hour, then stir with a fork to break up any ice crystals.
5. Continue freezing for an additional hour or until the sorbet reaches the desired consistency.
6. Scoop into bowls or serve in lemon halves for a charming presentation.

Nutritional Values (per serving):
- Calories: 120
- Fat: 0g
- Carbs: 32g

Protein: 0

Conclusion:

As we wrap up this culinary journey through the vibrant and healthful Mediterranean diet, I hope you've not only discovered a rich tapestry of flavors but also embraced a lifestyle that promotes well-being and longevity. The Mediterranean diet extends beyond a mere collection of recipes; it's a celebration of fresh, wholesome ingredients, cultural diversity, and the joy of savoring each bite. By incorporating the key principles outlined in this cookbook, you've not only nourished your body but also connected with the traditions and wisdom of Mediterranean cultures.

Remember, the Mediterranean diet is more than just a meal plan; it's a holistic approach to living. Its origins steeped in history and cultural significance have provided us with a roadmap to wellness. As we bid farewell to this culinary adventure, I encourage you to continue exploring, experimenting, and making these dishes a part of your daily life. Whether you're enjoying a leisurely breakfast, a vibrant salad, or a hearty seafood dinner, may each recipe bring you closer to the Mediterranean spirit – a celebration of life, good food, and the company of loved ones.

May your culinary endeavors be filled with joy, good health, and the unmistakable flavors of the Mediterranean.

Buon appetito!

MEASUREMENTS CONVERSION CHART

CUP	OUNCES	MILLIMETERS	TABLESPOONS
8 cups	64 oz	1895 ml	128
6 cups	48 oz	1420 ml	96
5 cups	40 oz	1180 ml	80
4 cups	32 oz	960 ml	64
2 cups	16 oz	480 ml	32
1 cup	8 oz	240 ml	16
¾ cup	6 oz	177 ml	12
⅔ cup	5 oz	158 ml	11
½ cup	4 oz	118 ml	8
⅜ cup	3 oz	90 ml	6
⅓ cup	2.4 oz	79 ml	5.5
¼ cup	2 oz	59 ml	4
⅛ cup	1 oz	30 ml	3
1/16 cup	½ oz	15 ml	1

30 DAY MEAL PLAN

	Breakfast	Lunch	Dinner
1	Mediterranean Avocado Toast	Mediterranean Lemon-Garlic Shrimp Pasta	Mediterranean Chickpea Salad
2	Greek Yogurt Parfait with Fresh Berries	Spaghetti Aglio e Olio with Olives and Tomatoes	Mediterranean Three-Bean Salad
3	Shakshuka with Feta	Lemon Garlic Herb Quinoa	Greek Chickpea and Spinach Casserole
4	Spinach and Feta Omelette	Greek Pasta Salad with Cherry Tomatoes and Feta	Spinach and Artichoke Orzo Salad
5	Olive and Tomato Focaccia	Tomato and Basil Farro Risotto	Herbed Couscous with Roasted Vegetables
6	Whole Wheat Mediterranean Pancakes	Balsamic-Glazed Chicken Thighs	Mediterranean Brown Rice Pilaf
7	Fig and Walnut Overnight Oats	Greek Lentil Soup with Spinach	Roasted Red Pepper and Feta Hummus Wrap
8	Mediterranean Egg Muffins	Mediterranean Chicken Pesto Pasta	Spinach and Feta Phyllo Triangles
9	Quinoa Breakfast Bowl with Almonds and Honey	Spinach and Feta Stuffed Bell Peppers	Mediterranean Lentil and Vegetable Soup
10	Greek-style Breakfast Burrito	Grilled Mediterranean Salmon	Artichoke and Sun-Dried Tomato Stuffed Portobello Mushrooms
11	Orange and Almond Breakfast Couscous	Lemon-Herb Baked Cod	Lemon Herb Roasted Vegetable Quinoa Bowl
12	Labneh and Cucumber Bagel	Mediterranean Lamb Kebabs with Tzatziki	Spanakorizo (Greek Spinach and Rice)
13	Cherry Tomato and Basil Frittata	Lemon-Herb Bulgur Pilaf	Caponata: Sicilian Eggplant Salad
14	Almond Butter and Banana Smoothie Bowl	Roasted Red Pepper and Artichoke Penne	Mediterranean Chickpea and Eggplant Casserole
15	Mediterranean Breakfast Wrap	White Bean and Rosemary Hummus	Greek Spanakopita Quesadillas
16	Mediterranean Avocado Toast	Shrimp and Olive Linguine with Tomato Sauce	Roasted Vegetable and Feta Orzo Salad
17	Greek Yogurt Parfait with Fresh Berries	Mediterranean Stuffed Acorn Squash	Tomato and Olive Polenta Stacks
18	Fig and Walnut Overnight Oats	Rosemary and Garlic Roast Pork Tenderloin	Mediterranean Pita Bread Salad

19	Mediterranean Egg Muffins	Eggplant and Tomato Lentil Stew	Spinach and Mushroom Greek-Style Risotto
20	Quinoa Breakfast Bowl with Almonds and Honey	Olive and Sun-Dried Tomato Polenta	Greek Style Grilled Swordfish
21	Greek-style Breakfast Burrito	Moroccan Spiced Chicken Tagine	Spicy Harissa Prawns
22	Cherry Tomato and Basil Frittata	Garlic and Herb Shrimp Skewers	Sun-Dried Tomato and Basil Pesto Cavatappi
23	Almond Butter and Banana Smoothie Bowl	Mediterranean Stuffed Squid	Lemon and Herb Fettuccine with Grilled Vegetables
24	Mediterranean Breakfast Wrap	Baked Lemon Garlic Tilapia	Mediterranean Sausage and Eggplant Rigatoni
25	Olive and Tomato Focaccia	Turkey and Spinach Stuffed Bell Peppers	Cherry Tomato and Kalamata Olive Linguine
26	Whole Wheat Mediterranean Pancakes	Eggplant and Zucchini Moussaka	Lemon-Oregano Grilled Scallops
27	Fig and Walnut Overnight Oats	Spanakorizo (Greek Spinach and Rice)	Eggplant and Zucchini Moussaka
28	Mediterranean Egg Muffins	Roasted Red Pepper and Feta Hummus Wrap	Pistachio-Crusted Halibut
29	Greek-style Breakfast Burrito	Spinach and Feta Stuffed Shells	Shrimp and Feta Orzo Pilaf
30	Orange and Almond Breakfast Couscous	Chicken and Olive Cacciatore	Mediterranean Stuffed Bell Peppers with Quinoa and Chickpeas

Discover Your Culinary Companions:

Exclusive Bonuses Inside!

We're thrilled to present you with not one but two exceptional bonuses to complement your Mediterranean Diet Cookbook. Elevate your dining experience and spice up your culinary journey with these insightful guides:

Bonus 1: "Dining Out the Mediterranean Way" Navigate restaurant menus, balance health and enjoyment, and savor the social aspect of dining out while adhering to your Mediterranean diet.

Bonus 2: "Understanding Mediterranean Spices" Unlock the secrets of cumin's warmth, coriander's complexity, mint's invigoration, and more. Explore the stories, health benefits, and versatile applications of these culinary treasures.

To download your bonuses scan the QR code below and Enjoy your culinary exploration!

Thank you for choosing our cookbook. Here's to a flavorful journey through the Mediterranean diet!

Bon appétit!

Dear Reader,

Thank you for choosing "The Time-Saving Mediterranean Diet Cookbook for Busy Beginners." Your decision to explore the vibrant and wholesome world of the Mediterranean diet is the first step towards a healthier and more delicious lifestyle.

As an author, I am committed to providing valuable content that meets the needs of readers like you. To enhance the quality of future editions and support the book's visibility on Amazon, I would greatly appreciate your feedback.

If you find this book helpful, informative, or enjoyable, please consider leaving a 5 STARS REVIEW on Amazon. Your insights and experiences can assist other readers in making informed decisions and contribute to the success of this book.

To leave a review click the link below or Scan the QR code, it only takes a few seconds

Your feedback is incredibly valuable and plays a crucial role in shaping the book's journey. Thank you for taking the time to share your thoughts and for being an essential part of this community.

Wishing you a delightful and fulfilling journey through the flavors of the Mediterranean!

Warm regards,

Daniel Ortiz

RECIPES INDEX

Made in the USA
Las Vegas, NV
06 March 2024

86770381R00046